THE STEP–BY–STEP
SEWING COURSE

THE STEP–BY–STEP
SEWING COURSE
MORE THAN 100 PROJECTS

GENERAL EDITOR: KAREN HEMINGWAY

Published in 2005 by Silverdale Books
an imprint of Bookmart Ltd
Registered Number 2372865
Trading as Bookmart Ltd
Blaby Road
Wigston
Leicester LE18 4SE

ISBN 1-84509-157-4

Editorial and design by
Amber Books Ltd
Bradley's Close
74–77 White Lion Street
London N1 9PF
www.amberbooks.co.uk

Project Editor: Sarah Uttridge
Design: Hawes Design

PICTURE CREDITS:
All International Masters Publishing BV

Printed in Dubai

Contents

Sewing Techniques

Sewing can be fun and easy once you master some basic techniques. To get you started, this section looks at the essential tools and materials you will need and step-by-step instructions for achieving success. From selecting the right fabric and notions, to using the correct settings on your sewing machine, there's handy information galore.

Whether you are a sewing novice or an experienced sewer, it is well worth reading this section before embarking on your sewing project.

Before you begin: Equipment

You will need some basic equipment to complete these projects. Below are some of the items you will need. You can purchase this equipment at a crafts or fabric store. Be sure to make a list of what you need before you go shopping so you don't forget a vital piece of equipment that will prevent you from starting a project. Having the right tools for each project will make them easier to complete and save time and effort.

CUTTING TOOLS

Use dressmaker's shears, with a 7–8-in. (18–20-cm) blade, and pinking shears for cutting fabric; sewing scissors, with a 5–6-in. (13–15-cm) blade, for general sewing needs; and embroidery scissors, with a 3–4-in. (7.5–10-cm) blade for snipping threads and cutting into corners. Use a seam ripper, with care, for unpicking stitches. A craft knife or paper scissors are essential for cutting patterns. When cutting many identical layers or straight panels and strips, a rotary cutter and self-healing mat will make the job quicker and easier.

Pinking shears
These make zigzag edges to stop material from fraying easily. Use them for seams.

Embroidery scissors
Use for needlework and fine cutting jobs.

Dressmaker's shears
Although almost all the projects in this book do not use patterns, these shears are designed for cutting fabrics with a pattern.

Rotary cutter and mat
Used to cut fabric, particularly useful for quiltmaking. Make sure you use a good-quality mat to protect your tabletop.

Seam ripper
A special cutting tool designed to unpick seams quickly and easily. Useful if you make a mistake with the sewing machine.

NEEDLES AND THREADS

Choosing the right fabrics for a project is important, but it is just as important to use the right needle and thread for the fabrics you use. This will ensure that your projects will look more professional when they are finished. If you do not have a speciality store nearby, many sell tools (and fabrics) on the Internet, which is a good source of advice for beginners. Essentials include 100% cotton or cotton-wrapped polyester thread and hand- and machine-sewing needles in sizes to complement various fabric weights. Use sharps for wovens and ballpoints for knits. A needle threader is also useful.

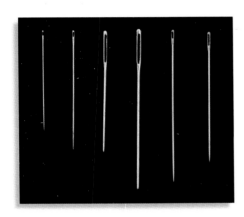

Needles

There are many types of needle available, and getting the right needle for your fabric is important. In general, a medium-length needle is suitable for most hand-sewing tasks. Sewing machines have their own needles for different fabrics—make sure you follow the machine manufacturer's own recommendations.

Threads

There are many different threads that can be bought, some for hand sewing and others for machine work. Ask in your local crafts or fabric store for advice—getting the right type of thread is as important as getting the right color!

PINNING ITEMS

Have on hand rustproof straight pins with flat or round heads, T-pins for heavy fabrics, and safety pins for quilting layers and threading casings.

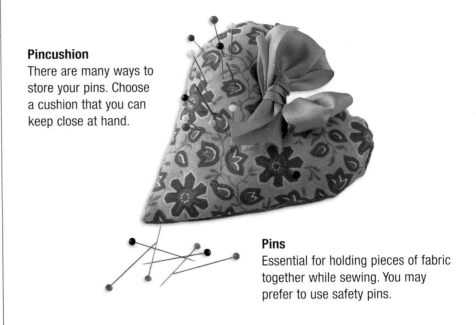

Pincushion

There are many ways to store your pins. Choose a cushion that you can keep close at hand.

Pins

Essential for holding pieces of fabric together while sewing. You may prefer to use safety pins.

MEASURING TOOLS

Use a flexible tape to measure yardage and curved or round objects. A clear ruler with grids is perfect for measuring off straight strips of fabric, and a yardstick can be used for measuring yardage and straight lines.

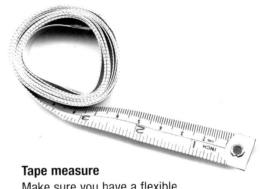

Tape measure

Make sure you have a flexible tape measure, not a metal one!

PRESSING TOOLS

A good steam iron with temperature controls, ironing board, and pressing cloth are essential for a professional finish.

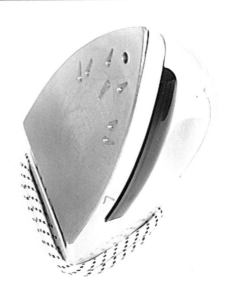

Iron

It may be necessary to press fabrics before you start sewing to remove any creases in the material. Make sure the iron is on the correct setting for the fabric you are pressing.

MARKING TOOLS

Tailor's chalk is handy for very temporary marks for notches, buttonholes, etc. Soft-lead pencils, disappearing markers, and dressmaker's carbon paper with a tracing wheel can all be used to mark out patterns and design lines. Test markers before use, as the various types react to fiber content, heat, and moisture in different ways.

Tailor's chalk
Use for marking guidelines on fabrics before cutting or sewing. The chalk can be brushed off later.

Marking pen
These special pens make marks that can either be washed out or will fade. Alternatively, you can use a chalk pencil.

HAND-SEWING TOOLS

There are items you can buy to make sewing easier and safer. A needle threader can save time and also prevent frustration.

Needle threader
A simple tool that helps thread a needle quickly and easily.

Thimble
This protects your thumb or finger when sewing by hand.

SEWING MACHINE ACCESSORIES

Your sewing machine will have different "feet" designed for different sewing tasks.

Sewing machine feet
Make sure you fit the correct foot for each task. Refer to your sewing machine manual for guidance on which foot to use.

Even the most accomplished sewer started out with a basic needle, thread, scissors, and a piece of fabric. Buy only what you need for each stage of the course, but buy the best tools you can afford.

BIAS TAPE

1. Use bias tape to finish shaped hems, make casings, and bind edges.
2. Bias tape is available in a variety of widths, so it can be used for many different projects. It has prefolded edges, and it stretches and shapes to fit curved areas.

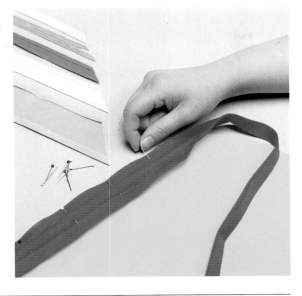

FUSIBLE WEB TAPE

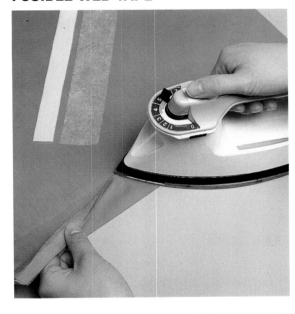

1. Fusible web tape is used to fuse two fabric layers together.
2. It is available in a wide range of widths or in sheets, sometimes with paper backing.
3. Always refer to manufacturer's instructions for use.

GROMMETS

1. Grommets are two-part metal units (grommet and washer) used to reinforce hole openings.
2. They are available in a wide range of sizes; larger sizes are particularly effective for using as a means to hang curtains.
3. Secure them with grommet pliers or use the tools in a grommet kit.

SPECIALIST TOOLS

These tools become more necessary as your sewing skills and devotion to the craft increase. The following are a few of the more frequently used tools.

- **Basting tape**, a double-sided adhesive, is needed when sewing slippery or hard-to-pin fabrics or for matching fabric across a seam. It should not be stitched over. Remove the tape after sewing, or if the fabric is washable, use water-soluble basting tape.

- **A combination point turner and button gauge** ensures uniformity. Use the point turner to push out corners on such items as pillows and place mats. Use the button gauge to space buttons evenly along the join and to form uniform thread shanks.

- **Bodkins** are shaped like long, blunt needles, and are used to thread elastic, ribbon, or cord through a casing or other opening.

- **Liquid seam sealant** helps prevent fabric fraying in small detail areas. It is also used to seal a cut edge.

- **A serger**, sometimes known as an overlock, can stitch, trim, and overcast in a single motion. A serger is used as a complement to the traditional sewing machine and cannot replace it. Sergers are ideal for making finished narrow seams, rolled hems, blindstitched hems and overcast seams; it can sew up to 1700 stitches per minute.

Know Your Sewing Machine

A sewing machine is a handy tool, providing creative opportunities from basic straight sewing to making buttonholes or elaborate quilts and embroidery—all at the flick of a switch or quick program.

Whether you buy a new sewing machine or a previously owned one, you should take time to familiarize yourself with the machine and practice using the different features. The more you familiarize yourself with it, the easier it will be to use.

The best way to get to know your sewing machine is to carefully read the manufacturer's manual. The position of the sewing machine parts is different with each manufacturer, so the picture below is for general information only.

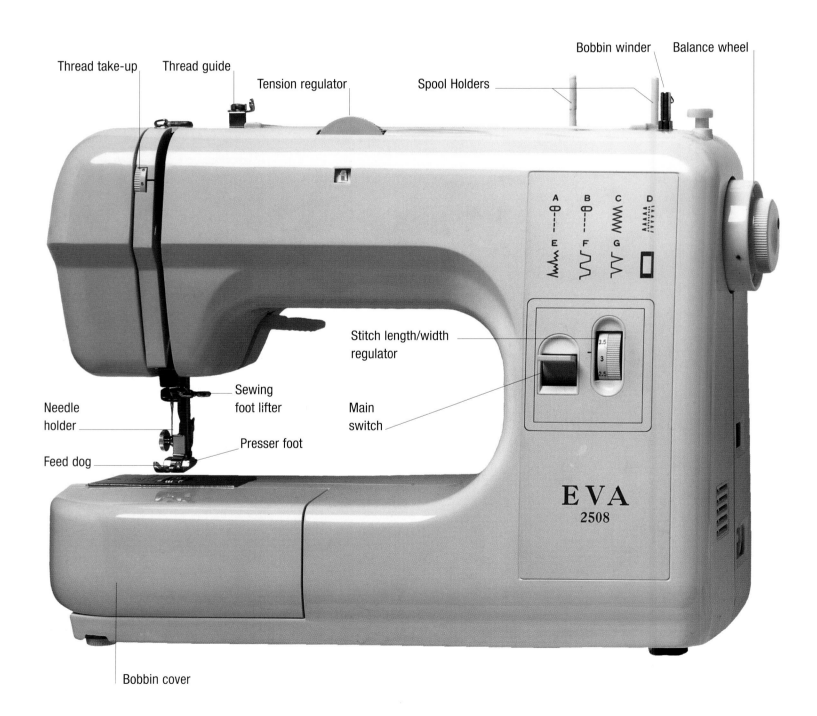

Thread take-up · Thread guide · Tension regulator · Bobbin winder · Balance wheel · Spool Holders · Stitch length/width regulator · Sewing foot lifter · Main switch · Needle holder · Presser foot · Feed dog · Bobbin cover

EVA
2508

THREADING A BOBBIN

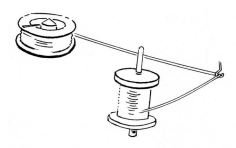

1. The lower thread needs to be evenly wound on the bobbin so that the machine sews with an even tension. To automatically wind the bobbin, you should refer to your sewing machine manual.

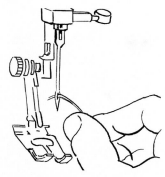

2. Thread the top thread through the guides and regulators on the sewing machine according to your manual. Raise the needle to thread it and insert the thread from the front to the back.

ADJUSTING THE TENSION

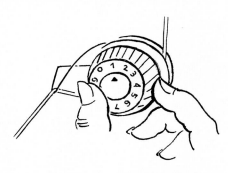

1. If the tension needs correcting, adjust the tension regulator first. Turn the dial higher to increase the tension of the top thread and lower to decrease it.

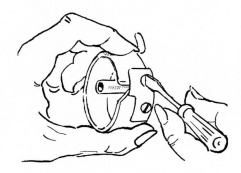

2. To correct the tension further, adjust the tension spring on the bobbin. Turn the screw clockwise to increase tension on the lower thread and counterclockwise to decrease it.

visible. Then gently pull the bottom thread to release the end.

Set the stitch length you require. To start sewing, place the work under the needle and lower the presser foot. Hold both threads to the back of the work to prevent the thread from tangling, until you have sewn a few stitches. To secure the thread, sew a few stitches backward along the stitch line to the starting point (your manual may suggest other methods). Then start sewing at a steady pace. The machine will feed the fabric, so lightly guide the fabric without pulling it. To finish, secure the threads with a few more backstitches.

It is important to ensure that your sewing machine is set up correctly before you begin. Make sure you read the manual carefully and follow the manufacturer's advice.

You don't need a very sophisticated sewing machine for most craft or home-decorating projects, so consider your needs before you invest in a new machine. An old one that produces a sturdy straight stitch and a zigzag stitch will get you started. If you want to buy a new machine, go to a reputable dealer so that you can see different models demonstrated and try it yourself. Choose one that you find easy to thread and to operate, that isn't too heavy to lift, and that offers flexible controls for tension and stitch length.

Make sure your machine is always kept in good working order. Have it serviced and oiled as recommended by the manufacturer. Read the manual carefully so you know exactly how to

use the machine properly, and always sew with a sharp needle.

Getting started

Insert a needle that is suitable for your project; fine needles are essential for lightweight fabrics such as silks and ginghams, and thicker needles are needed for heavy fabrics like woolens and velvets.

Referring to the manual, thread the top thread around the machine and through the needle. Wind the bobbin and insert it in the machine. Hold the end of the top thread in your left hand and slowly turn the balance wheel so that the needle descends and comes up again. Gently pull the top thread so that a loop of the bottom thread is

Checking the tension

It is very important to sew with an even tension so that the stitches do not ravel and the fabric does not pucker. Always test the tension first on scraps of your project fabric, with the same number of layers.

If the tension is correct, the stitches look the same on both the right and the wrong sides. When the top tension is too tight, the top thread is stretched out and the lower thread makes loops on the right side. The same effect occurs on the wrong side if the bottom tension is too tight.

On a new machine or after servicing, the bobbin tension should be properly set, so you should adjust the top tension regulator first (see box above).

Basic techniques

If you are a complete beginner, you'll need to learn these basic skills before you start your sewing course. Poor preparation for sewing can ruin an entire project—time spent planning and measuring your fabric accurately is never wasted. It is also important to use plenty of pins to keep two pieces of fabric correctly aligned while you are sewing, especially when machine sewing. A mistake can take a long time to correct!

When selecting sewing thread, use cotton-covered polyester or 100% cotton for general sewing, and rayon, metallic, and other novelty threads for decorative effects.

PRESSING

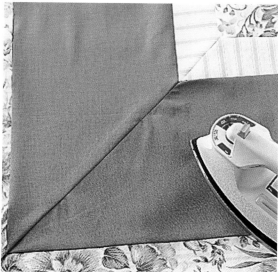

1. Select a steam iron with multiple fabric settings.
2. Follow the manufacturer's recommendations for temperature and steam setting for the fabric you have chosen.
3. Use a pressing cloth with delicate fabrics such as silks to protect them from heat damage.

MEASURING

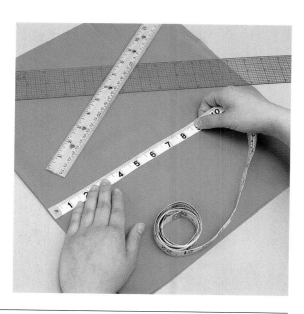

1. To measure up for the projects accurately, use a flexible tape measure for measuring surfaces, taking furniture measurements, gauging angles, and establishing square and bias of fabrics. Try to take measurements on a flat surface if possible.
2. Use wooden and clear grid-marked rulers for accuracy and as a rotary cutting guide to give a straight edge.

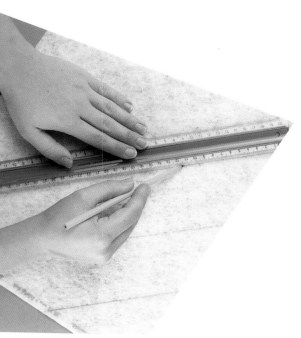

Always press the fabric and then pull it tight when you are measuring and marking. This will make your measurements more accurate and help prevent any expensive mistakes. Don't be afraid to double-check your calculations, and if you use a special marking pen or tailor's chalk, you can easily rub out any marks that are wrong. With difficult measurements, always cut off less than you think necessary; then trim off the excess in small amounts until you have the shape you require. Measuring and cutting fabric are difficult at first, but with practice you will soon be an expert!

FINISHING OFF EDGES

1. To cut edges, carefully use a rotary cutter for heavy fabrics and layers. Make sure you use a thick cutting mat to protect your furniture.
2. Pinking shears produce a zigzag edge that helps prevent fraying, but you can also use dressmaker's shears for general cutting.
3. Once you have finished an edge, use snippers or embroidery scissors to cut off any loose thread ends.

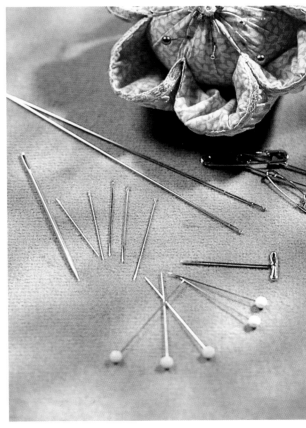

To aid sewing, use rustproof pins and needles in a thickness that suits the weight of the fabric. Pick sharp points (called sharps) for wovens and ballpoints for knits.

PINNING

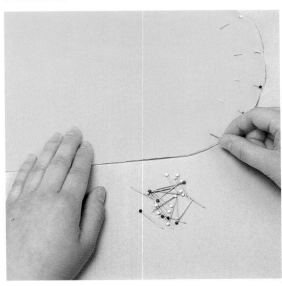

1. Use straight pins to hold fabric layers together or indicate markings. Safety pins can be used but are harder to adjust easily.
2. Place the pins at a right angle to the seam line with their heads to the right of the presser foot on your sewing machine.
3. Be sure to use enough pins to hold the fabrics in place and prevent the layers from shifting.

USING PATTERNS

1. Although most of the projects in this book do not use patterns, once you are experienced at sewing, you may wish to buy a project pattern from a crafts store. First cut out the pattern carefully, and lay this over the fabric you have chosen to use. Alternatively, use a dressmaker's carbon paper.
2. A tracing wheel makes it easy to transfer marks from pattern to fabric.
3. Water-soluble and air-evaporating marking pens can be used on most fabrics. Mark the side that won't be seen on the finished project.
4. Use tailor's chalk on delicate fabrics.

Keep your needles safely stored during a project by using a pincushion. That way, if the telephone rings, you can easily find your needle after the call is over. On page 64 you can find out how to make your own!

Machine Sewing

Make sure your projects look professional by practicing the basic stitches and seams, and learning how to get the most from your sewing machine. Here are some of the basic stitches and techniques to get you started, along with some useful tips on selecting the right needles and threads for the job.

MACHINE SEWING GUIDE

Fabric	Thread	Needle	Stitch Length
Delicate nets, fine lace, organdy, lawn, voile	Mercerized cotton, no. 50, fine polyester, silk	60–70 sharp, 70 ballpoint for synthetics	0.04 in.–0.06 in. (1–1.5 mm)
Lightweight percale, dotted Swiss, broderie anglaise, lace, semisheer curtain nets, linen, fine denims	Mercerized cotton, no. 50, fine polyester-cotton, fine polyester, silk	80 sharp	0.04 in.–0.08 in. (1.5–2 mm)
Medium heavy brocade, damask, satin, velveteen, medium-weight corduroy, hopsacking, felt	Mercerized cotton, no. 40, polyester-cotton, polyester	80–90 sharp, 80–90 ballpoint for knits	0.08 in.–0.10 in. (2–2.5 mm)
Heavyweight velvet, wide-ribbed corduroy, burlap, canvas, tapestry ticking, sailcloth	Heavy-duty polyester-cotton, heavy-duty polyester	90–110 sharp	0.01 in.–0.12 in. (2.5–3 mm)

BASIC MACHINE SEAMS

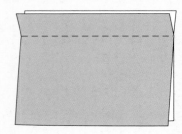

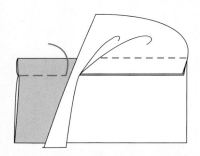

Plain seam
Pin the right sides together with pins at right angles to the raw edges. Place the fabric in the machine with the bulk to the left of needle and the raw edges to the right. Sew, removing the pins as you go. Backstitch at the beginning and end to secure thread. Press open.

French seam
Pin the wrong sides of fabric together and stitch ½ in. (10 mm) from the raw edges. Trim the seam allowance to

⅛ in. (3 mm). Fold the fabric right sides together, rolling the seam to bring stitching to the fold line. Press flat. Stitch ¼ in. (5 mm) from the fold to encase the raw edges. Press.

Welt seam
Sew plain seam and press both seam allowances to one side. Trim inner seam allowance to ¼ in. (5 mm). Sew along one side of seam, catching the wider seam allowance.

Stitching straight lines
There are many aids available to help you sew straight lines. Some attach to the sewing machine bed and others to the presser foot. There is even a tear-away paper marked at 1/4-in. (5-mm) intervals, which can be stitched over and then torn off the fabric.

Stitching around curves
Shorten stitch length and set machine to a slower speed. Guide fabric under needle for an even seam allowance.

Stitching around corners
When you reach a corner, stop machine with needle in fabric. Lift foot, pivot fabric, lower foot, and continue.

SEWING STRAIGHT-STITCH SEAMS

1. Use a straight stitch for seams.
2. Sew along the seam line, avoiding any basting stitches if possible.
3. Remove any pins as you go. Alternatively, you could use an adjustable edge guide or the edge of the presser foot as a guide for the seam allowance.

SEWING ZIGZAG STITCHES

1. A close zigzag stitch is useful for adding strength to seams or decoration to your projects. It is also perfect for keeping the raw edges of appliqué shapes neat.
2. First baste the shapes to the background fabric.
3. Then zigzag steadily around the shape, making sure the raw edges are covered and pivoting on the needle to turn around awkward angles.

SEWING GATHERED TAPE

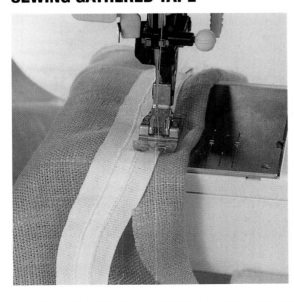

1. To sew in gathering or pleater tape, turn under 1 in. (2.5 cm) from the top raw edge; press.
2. Cut tape 2 in. (5 cm) longer than the curtain width.
3. Press under 1 in. (2.5 cm) at each end of the tape.
4. Pin and baste the tape ½ in. (1 cm) down from the fold. Stitch along all edges of the tape.

TRY THIS!

The more you sew, the more your confidence will grow and you will find easier ways to get professional results. Try out the different attachments and decorative stitches that your machine offers and also experiment with these tips.

- Set the machine for a wide zigzag to secure hook-and-loop tape, or to encase shirring elastic or narrow ribbon.
- Experiment with any automatic decorative stitches on your machine. A simple linear stitch can be used to add effective detail to bed and table linens. Try matching thread to add texture or contrasting thread for a more dramatic impact.

DECORATIVE STITCHES

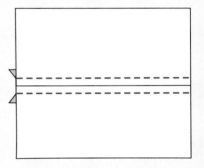

Topstitch

Use this simple stitch to decorate and reinforce a seam or edge. Press open the seam or edge. On the right side of the fabric, work a line of stitches an equal distance from the seam or edge, catching any seam allowance. For double topstitching, work stitching on each side of seam, an equal distance from it.

Zigzag

Neaten raw edges along seams and attach ribbons and trimmings with this automatic stitch. Set the machine for closer stitches to give a neat finish to appliqué shapes.

Hand Sewing

You can hand stitch when you do not have access to a sewing machine or when your sewing project requires a more delicate touch. Stitch in the direction that is most comfortable for you, right to left or left to right.

When choosing a needle, choose one that is small enough to easily slide into the fabric but large enough not to bend or break. Use needles with large eyes for thick or multiple-thread strands. It is a good idea to wear a thimble when hand stitching, to protect your fingers.

Choosing a Needle

To stitch by hand, use sharp needles, sized 1–12, for general sewing. A higher number indicates a finer needle, which should be used on lightweight fabrics. If you want to sew knitted material, choose a blunt needle.

Choosing Thread

The heavier the weight of the thread, the stronger it is, but the stitching will be more visible. Choose a thick thread for decoration or heavy fabrics. Fine thread is best suited to lightweight fabrics, but the stitching will not be as strong. If you can, take a sample of the fabric you wish to use to your crafts store to get the best color match you can—unless you want to show off your stitching, of course!

To add strength to thread and prevent it from knotting while sewing by hand, run the thread through beeswax housed in a slotted container. These are available from specialty stores.

BASIC SEAMS   *Note: Blue shows the wrong side of the fabric.*

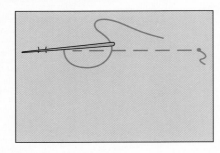

Basting

A temporary stitch used to hold pieces of fabric together more securely than pinning. Working from right to left, take several stitches onto the needle before pulling it through the fabric. Stitches can be large and unevenly spaced for most fabrics. Make stitches smaller and space them evenly to secure curved seams or smooth fabrics.

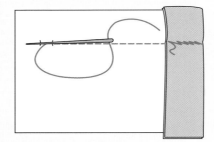

Backstitch

The strongest hand stitch, used where machine stitching would be difficult. Bring the needle and thread through the fabric to the top. Insert the needle about ⅛ in. (3 mm) behind the point where it emerged; then bring it out at the same distance in front. Repeat, inserting needle where the stitch ended. Be sure to keep the stitches even.

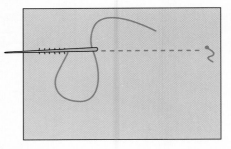

Running stitch

This permanent stitch is used for gathering fabrics, making tucks, and also mending. Working from right to left, weave the needle in and out of the fabric a few times before pulling the thread through. Be sure to keep both the stitches and the spaces small and even.

To gather fabric, work two parallel rows of slightly longer running stitches. Securely holding one of the threads, push the fabric along it to form even gathers. When the fabric is the right length, fasten off the thread.

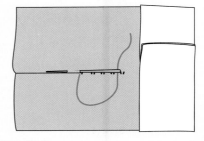

Slipstitch

Also known as slip hemming. This is a barely visible stitch used for hemming. Working from right to left, bring the needle and thread up through the fold. Take a stitch into the fabric directly opposite this point, catching only one or two threads. Slip the needle back through the fold for about ¼ in. (5 mm), then pull out and repeat the stitch.

THREADING

1. Threading a needle can be tricky, and some people may struggle with it. Here is the best way to do it.
2. With a sharp pair of scissors, cut the end of the thread at a 45° angle.
3. Hold the needle so the eye of the needle is open toward you.
4. Slip the thread into the needle.
5. Knot one end of the thread, leaving one end loose to sew with.

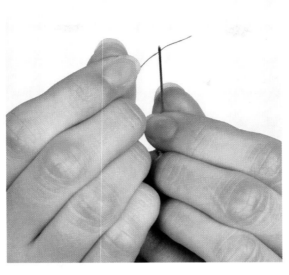

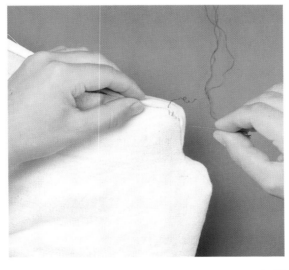

SEWING

1. Pull the thread through the eye far enough to create a tail that is 3–4 in. (7.5–10 cm). This end remains unknotted.
2. Having a long enough tail will prevent the thread from coming out of the needle while you are sewing.

Some projects, such as cushion and duvet covers, require fasteners—buttons, zippers, or ribbons. Although there are specialist tools to attach fasteners and decorations, many people attach these by hand. Buttons are often used as decorations themselves.

SEWING ON BUTTONS

1. To sew buttons, backstitch on the placement mark with double thread; position button on fabric and stitch through the holes.
2. Carefully lift the button from fabric; wind extra thread around the stitches, known as the shank, to add strength.
3. Finally, backstitch and secure the thread ends.

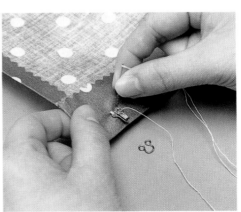

As an alternative to buttons, more experienced sewers might try using hook-and-eye fasteners for their duvet covers or chair covers. To install a hook and eye, sew the hook to the wrong side 1/16 in. (2 mm) from edge, taking several stitches through each hole and around the end of the hook. Position the loop of the curved eye a little beyond the opposite edge; stitch through the holes to hold the eye flat.

Selecting Fabric

The success of any craft or home-decorating project depends on the suitability of the chosen fabric's color, weight, texture, and fiber content.

Manufacturers often design home-decorating fabrics to work well as part of a collection, making it easy to mix and match. Take some samples home to view in your own surroundings. Above all, choose fabrics you love.

This section looks at how to choose fabric and how to prepare the fabric before starting your project. It is important to know how to correctly cut the fabric and finish off the edges for your project to be a complete success.

Certain fabrics are more suited to some projects, so be sure your fabric is suitable for your chosen project before you make a purchase.

A little textile knowledge and also some helpful shopping tips can make choosing the right fabric for your sewing project much less daunting.

Guidelines for Selecting Fabric

Always refer to any project instructions for suggested fabrics.

- Closely woven fabrics, such as cottons and cotton blends, are most suitable for sewing small pieces because they do not fray excessively.
- Avoid knits that stretch too much. Stable knits are fine for the smaller projects, such as pillow covers.
- Heavyweight fabrics, such as suede and leather, are suitable for large projects. However, their bulk makes sewing small details and narrow seam allowances difficult.
- Textured fabrics, such as fleece, corduroy, velvet, and brocade, can obscure design details.
- Match the scale of printed designs to the size of the project. Small pillow covers, for example, look best with small designs, while big pillows can carry larger motifs.
- To test the stability of the weave, rub a fingernail over the fabric; if the threads do not separate, the fabric has a good, tight weave.
- To check fabric resiliency, crumble a small section of the fabric in your hand; if it returns to its original state, it is both wrinkle resistant and resilient.
- To ensure color uniformity, buy all the amount needed from one bolt.

There is an amazing variety of home-decorating and craft fabrics, ranging from lightweight cotton and synthetics to heavier canvas and tapestries. These fabrics can be used to make curtains and linens, table and chair covers, or linings for baskets.

FABRIC DIRECTORY

Fabric	Description	Uses	Care
Broadcloth	Fine, tightly woven, with slight rib	Used for window treatments and most other crafts	Machine washable
Chintz	Closely woven, with glazed surface	Used for window treatments, slipcovers, and other home-decorating projects	Machine washable, but glazed finish washes out over time
Eyelet	Fabric with an embroidered-and-openwork design	Used for curtains and feminine-style accessories	Machine washable; to press, cover surface with towel, press fabric wrong side up
Gingham	Lightweight plain weave, with a checked or plaid pattern	Used for all types of home-decorating and craft projects	Machine washable
Lace	Openwork fabric with many different designs and textures; made from cotton, silk, synthetics, and blends	Used for window treatments, pillows, bed linens; lace trims, flat or pregathered, used for edgings on home-decorating projects	Care depends on fiber content; check bolt; press lace wrong side up with press cloth
Taffeta	Smooth, crisp, plain weave with luster; made of silk, acetate, rayon, nylon, polyester, or blends	Used for window treatments, table decor, clothing and pillows; does not wear well	Care depends on fiber content; check bolt
Velvet	Luxurious, with short pile; made from silk, rayon, nylon, or cotton	Used for drapes, upholstery, pillows, and other accessories	Care depends on fiber content; check bolt

FABRIC KNOW-HOW

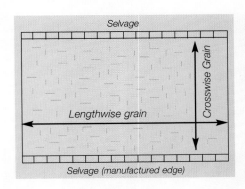

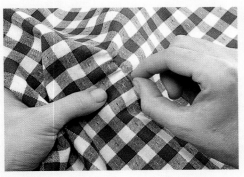

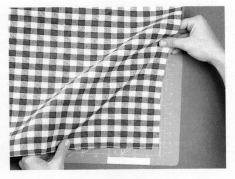

The grain line

Grain line defines direction of fabric threads. Lengthwise grain is parallel to selvage. Crosswise grain runs from selvage to selvage. Buy fabrics on grain with crosswise threads at right angles to lengthwise threads.

Finding the grain

Pull one crosswise thread from selvage to selvage until fabric puckers. Cut across fabric on this thread. The newly cut edge should be at an exact right angle to selvage.

Straightening the grain

Fabric is off grain if the newly cut edges are misaligned when fabric is folded lengthwise with selvages even. To straighten grain, pull fabric diagonally until threads are at right angles to each other at opposite corners.

FABRIC GUIDELINES

It is essential to use the right fabric for the right job, so be sure to read the manufacturer's tag before making a purchase.

As a general guide, fabrics used for upholstery should be strong, with a tight weave, to withstand wear and tear. Fabrics are tested for fire resistance and wear and can be treated to make them stain-resistant, too. It may also be worth considering how often they will need cleaning, especially if the fabric must be dry-cleaned. You will find that most fabrics are sold in widths of 47 in. (120 cm) or 54 in. (137 cm), but some are available in widths of up to 55 in. (140 cm). Sheeting fabrics are generally sold in widths of 90 in. (228 cm) or 110 in. (280 cm).

Fibers

Natural fibers, such as cotton, linen, wool, and silk, are hard-wearing. Cotton and linen are often mixed with synthetic fibers to make them softer or easier to care for. Wool is mixed with cotton, silk, or linen to stop it from shrinking. Silk is expensive but drapes beautifully. Man-made fibers are inexpensive and usually easy-care. Polyester is wrinkle-free and does not fade in sunlight. Viscose/acetate is soft and silky and drapes well. Man-made fibers are also used to re-create traditional finishes, such as viscose damask or rayon moiré.

Colors

When choosing colors, remember that cool colors (blues and greens) recede, while warm colors (reds and yellows) pop out. Dark colors and bright colors tend to dominate. A small amount of dark fabric will have more impact than a large amount of light fabric.

PREPARING FABRIC

1. Launder and press all washable material before cutting to allow for initial shrinkage, to remove sizing, and to be sure the fabric stays on grain after it has been washed.
2. Press while still slightly damp.
3. When dry, check that the fabric was not pulled off grain.

CUTTING FABRIC

1. Fabrics with one-way print designs, nap, pile, and lustrous surfaces have special cutting needs.
2. Check selvages for arrows indicating cutting direction. Always cut sections of napped and shiny fabric in the same direction, so light reflects evenly.

TRIMMING SELVAGES

1. Trim selvages away before cutting out fabric.
2. If the fabric is directional, mark the direction on the back.
3. Use a rotary cutter, see-through rule, and cutting mat to trim selvages quickly and cleanly.

PREVENTING EDGES FROM RAVELING

Use pinking shears, liquid fray preventer, or seam sealant along the cut edges of fabric. If you use liquid fray preventer, make sure you protect your work surface before you begin.

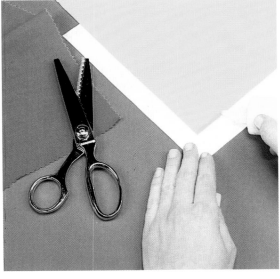

FINISHING SEAMS

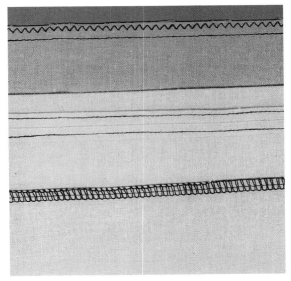

1. Finish seams to neaten and strengthen your project. Zigzag-stitch between the seam and raw edges.
2. Turn the raw edges to the wrong side and stitch along the folded edge.
3. Use an overlock stitch to encase the raw edges. An alternative option is to buy a serger, a special machine for finishing seams that cuts away excess material while overedging the seam at the same time.

By choosing the right fabric, you can create some wonderful effects around your home. This light, flowing material on these curtains creates a Mediterranean, summery feel.

WHAT IS BIAS?

Woven fabric has fixed threads (warp) that are interlaced at right angles by filler threads (weft). The warp is the lengthwise grain, which runs parallel to the selvages; the weft is the weaker crosswise grain, which has more give. The bias has the most stretch of all. Fabric cut at a 45° angle to the selvage is very flexible; bias strips are ideal for binding corners on raw edges or covering piping cord. Join strips at the short ends, with right sides together in a V-shape, matching any pattern. Open out the seam and trim allowance. Press the seam open.

To cut bias strips, mark lines at a 45° angle to the selvage.

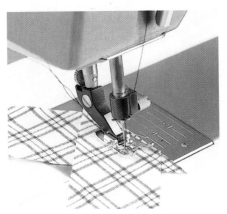

Machine stitch bias strips together in a V-shape.

Matching Patterned Fabric

Fabrics with large-scale prints, plaids, or stripes require careful matching for harmonious and visually balanced results. A mismatched seam detracts from the entire appearance of any project.

Extra yardage is necessary to match prints, so planning and piecing before cutting is important. As a general rule, measure the length of the pattern repeat and buy extra fabric equal to one repeat multiplied by each seam or panel that needs to be matched.

In addition to pattern repeats, many prints are directional, which means they feature an up-and-down or side-to-side print and therefore require a "with nap" layout, one in which each fabric piece is cut out in the same direction. Once you have determined the necessary yardage, plan cutting carefully to avoid waste and to ensure a visually pleasing product.

Choosing fabrics is fun, but while pattern fabrics bring color and interest to your sewing projects, they also bring potential problems. Remember to think about the other colors in the room you are creating the project for—will your new curtains or pillows match your overall color scheme?

Whether you like loud, outrageous patterns or more reserved, calmer fabrics, there is something for everyone. A vital part of choosing fabric for curtains or a bedspread is that you correctly match the pattern. An incorrectly matched pattern can look unsightly. Follow the tips opposite to produce a professional-looking result for your patterned projects.

CHECKING THE PATTERN

1. Look on the selvage for marks indicating the beginning and end of a repeat, or measure the size of a repeat.
2. Selvages on directional prints also have arrows indicating which end is up.
3. Copy the markings onto the back of the fabric before cutting off the selvage.

MATCHING THE PATTERN

1. Cut out the fabric sections so that the top edge of each is at same point on the print.
2. Trim off the selvages.
3. Turn under ¾ in. (2 cm) along the matching raw edge of one piece, then pin and press the folded edge with an up-and-down motion.

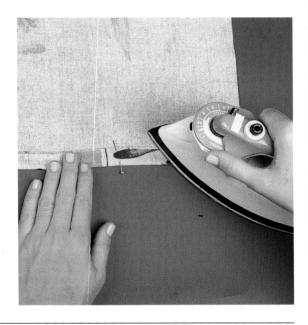

JOINING THE PATTERN TOGETHER

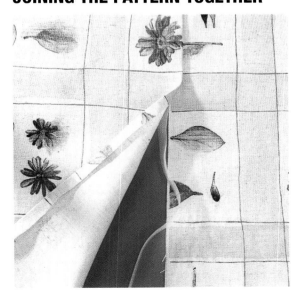

1. Place double-faced basting tape on the right side of the adjoining piece, along the seam line.
2. Pin the pieces together, aligning the printed pattern and sandwiching tape.
3. Stitch the seam from wrong side, but do not stitch through the tape.
4. Once you have finished the seam, carefully remove the tape.

POPULAR WEAVES

- **Satin weave**, a smooth, silky fabric ideal for curtains or upholstery.

- **Twill**, a firm-weave fabric, usually with diagonal ribbed stripes, which is tough and durable enough to be used for heavy-duty upholstery.

- **Jacquard**, made on a special loom with woven patterns on one side of the fabric. Used for covering stools, curtains, and cushions.

- **Damask**, a reversible-patterned Jacquard.

- **Sheeting**, plain woven cotton or polyester-cotton mix mostly used for bedding, cushions, and curtains.

- **Chintz**, a glazed or polished cotton, used for curtains, valances, blinds, bedspreads, and cushions.

- **Lace** and **net**, open-weave patterned fabrics mostly used for curtains and tablecloths.

Beginner Projects

This section will get you started on some easier projects that are ideal for the beginner. You can try making some stylish tiebacks for your curtains or add your own decorative touch to customize your next shower curtains.

Impress your friends by making eye-catching pillows or a fabulous cover for an old table. Although these projects are simple, they can make a wonderful difference to your home.

Beginner Techniques

In this section, you will find lots of projects that will give you maximum impact—even while you are still learning the basic techniques. You'll be surprised how easy it is to make stunning curtains, decorative tiebacks, and stylish shades to grace your windows. You can also try simple ideas for finishing the edges of throw blankets or make beautiful tablecloths, runners, and place mats, or elegant pillows.

You can also try applying appliqués on a shower curtain or making a log-cabin patchwork pillow. Try a few projects in this section and you'll soon have the confidence to dip into the following sections. For easy reference, the techniques are listed in the order that you find them in the book.

The ideas here will give you practice in the basic skills for sewing and help you build a repertoire that you can apply to any home-decorating project. You will discover hours of enjoyment and produce items you are really proud of!

HOW TO MAKE A ROD CASING

1. Fold top edge of the panel to wrong side by ½ in. (1 cm).
2. Measure around the rod, then halve the measurement and add 1¼ in. (3 cm) for the heading and ease.
3. Fold fabric over again by the new measurement.
4. Press. Sew along bottom fold and ¾ in. (2 cm) below top fold.

USING GROMMETS

1. You can use grommets to make shower curtains and other simple drapes. Lay the panel wrong side up.
2. Push the front of the grommet up through the hole in the fabric.
3. Place the grommet back over the front shaft.
4. Insert the grommet tool, and hammer the tool to flatten the front shaft.

This zingy room divider demonstrates what amazing results can be achieved by mixing and matching crisp cotton fabrics. You can easily create many looks using different patterns.

HOW TO USE FUSIBLE WEB FOR APPLIQUÉ

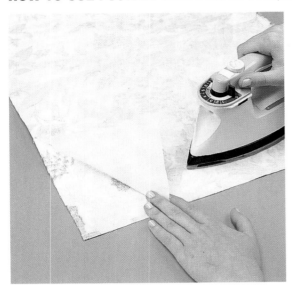

1. Fusible web bonds fabrics and stops the raw edges from raveling.
2. Following the manufacturer's instructions, iron the paper-backed web to the back of the uncut appliqué fabric.
3. Cut out and peel off the paper.
4. Fuse the appliqué to the background.

Add a total new look to an old shower curtain by adding fabric appliqués.

USING HOOK-AND-LOOP TAPE ON PILLOW COVERS

1. Hook-and-loop tape makes a very effective closure on pillow covers and is easy to sew in and to use.
2. Cut both sides of the tape to length.
3. Attach them to fabric by stitching along all four edges.

SEWING A POINTED BORDER

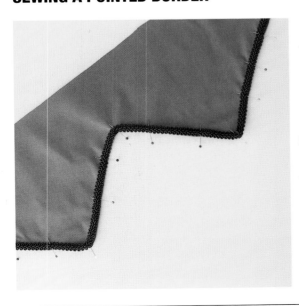

1. To make interesting blinds, you may want to make a pointed border. Cut two fabric pieces to same width as shade by desired depth, plus 1 in. (2.5 cm).
2. Mark desired shape along one long edge; cut out.
3. With right sides together, stitch along the sides and shaped edge; turn and press.
4. Stitch trim along the shaped border edge.

Bring some interest into your room by adding a blind with a creative design. You can use the same pattern on other items to create a wonderful effect and also a talking point.

HOW TO JOIN FABRIC PATTERNS

1. To join patterned fabric together, fold under seam allowance of one panel and press.
2. With right sides facing up, position folded edge of panel over selvage edge of matching panel, align design, and pin.
3. Repin with right sides together, then stitch together.

HOW TO MAKE CIRCULAR SHAPES

1. For a large circular shape, fold the fabric in half, and in half again.
2. Holding one end of a tape measure at the double-folded corner and using tailor's chalk, mark the radius of the desired shape to make an arc.
3. Cut along the line through all four layers of fabric.

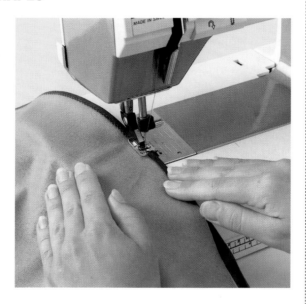

HOW TO MAKE A GEOMETRIC RUNNER

1. Mark and cut out geometric runner.
2. Stitch together front and back, right sides facing, leaving a 3-in. (7.5-cm) opening.
3. Clip into seam allowances at inside corners; trim seam allowances at outer corners.
4. Turn right side out; press. Slipstitch opening closed.

ADDING EXTRAS

There are many ways in which you can decorate your sewing creations without spending lots of time. Try some of these ideas:

- Make your own tassels to add distinction to your shades and pillows. Choose colors of thread that match the fabric. You could use embroidery floss and even include some metallic threads.

- Piece together two fabrics to make your curtains or drapes. Sew the joining horizontal seam about two-thirds of the way down the panel. For the best coordinated effect, choose fabrics with the same color scheme—for example, take a plain fabric and pick out the color in a gingham.

- Add borders of ribbon or braid to the bottom edge of curtains and drapes. Use just one understated strip or more for an extravagant look. You could mix and match patterned and plain ribbons and braids for an eclectic feel, or use one type, such as velvet ribbon, in related colors for more sophistication.

- Make a heading with evenly spaced metal grommets and hang your curtain from a tension wire.

- Update existing pillows or give new ones a modern look by attaching buttons in a striking pattern. Keep it simple by sewing on five-by-five rows to make a square in the middle of the pillow front. Choose mother-of-pearl buttons for real chic and a plain subtly textured fabric, such as linen, to show them off.

THE COLOR WHEEL

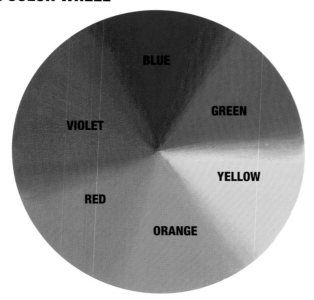

Colors that are close to neutral, like creams, beiges, and soft mineral shades, work well together or as a background to link other stronger statements. If you use them on their own, make sure you introduce plenty of texture for interest.

You can create a very harmonious scheme by combining colors that are close on the color wheel, such as blue with purple or red with orange. Harmonious they may be, but only the first combination will be restful. The second combination is best reserved for somewhere you want the mood to be powerful and energetic!

Colors that are opposite each other on the color wheel provide strong contrasts. They will tend to fight in similar proportions, but use a small accent of one against a background of its opposite, such as a red cushion in a green room, and your scheme will really come alive.

TIPS FOR SUCCESS!

- Check the items in the "You'll Need" box and gather together everything you need before you start. Make sure you have enough fabric for the whole project—there's nothing worse than running out in the middle!

- Choose the fabrics for your first projects with care. A stable fabric that is easy to handle, press, and launder is by far the easiest for beginners. Try a crisp cotton rather than a heavy velvet, flimsy synthetic, or brocade that ravels easily. A plain fabric or one with a small pattern will also be easier to match.

- Keep your equipment, especially your sewing machine, in good condition. Use sharp needles, change cutter blades, and have scissor blades sharpened regularly.

- Remember the importance of pressing each stage in order to achieve a really smart finish.

Curtains with Tab Headings

Adding tabs to the tops of curtain panels is one of the easiest ways to transform a simple window dressing into something special. It's no trouble to do and requires only a small amount of extra fabric.

Easy-to-sew tab tops create a cozy, informal, decorative finish for plain curtain panels. Finishing the top of unlined gingham curtain panels with loops or ties of fabric, rather than with the more conventional rod casing, gives the window a pleasant, airy look.

The wide loops of the tabs also make the curtain panels easier to hang and to draw. Let the curtain panels hang free or sweep the panels to one side and use a tieback to hold them open. Tabs made from the same fabric as the panels finish the curtains nicely.

Tie fabric strips into perky bows across the top width of curtain panels to give a fresh look with very little effort. For a refined, contemporary look, use a linen trim, instead of self-fabric for the tabs and for a matching decorative border.

Measuring for Curtains

Follow these guidelines to determine how much fabric you'll need to make the curtains and tabs.

- Measure from top of curtain rod to desired finished length. Use this as a base measurement.
- Before cutting, add ½ in. (1 cm) for top hem allowance and 2 in. (5 cm) for hem allowance at bottom; add 3 in. (7.5 cm) for width of tab strip and 2 in. (5 cm) for heading strip. For example, for a 40 in. (1 m)-wide curtain with a finished length of 50 in. (1.27 m), you will need 57½ in. (1.46 m) of 45 in. (1.14 m)-wide fabric: 50 in. (1.27 m) plus ½ in. (1 cm) plus 2 in. (5 cm) plus 3 in. (7.5 cm) plus 2 in. (5 cm).
- Bows for tabs will require an additional ½ yd. (45 cm) of fabric.

Preliminary Sewing

Cut strips of fabric for the curtain tabs and complete hems for curtain panels.

- Using a ruler and tailor's chalk, carefully draw a line across full width of fabric 2 in. (5 cm) up from bottom and another line 3 in. (7.5 cm) above first line. Cut fabric along these lines to make two separate strips. On long edge of 2 in. (5 cm)-wide strip, press under ½ in. (1 cm) to wrong side; set strip aside.
- On bottom edge of curtain piece, turn under 1 in. (2.5 cm) to wrong side and press. Turn under 1 in. (2.5 cm) again and press. Open out turned-under edges.

NOTE: All the seams for the curtain are sewn with ½ in. (5 cm) seam allowances unless otherwise noted.

You'll Need:

- ✓ Curtain fabric & matching sewing thread
- ✓ Tape measure & ruler
- ✓ Scissors
- ✓ Straight & safety pins
- ✓ Sewing machine
- ✓ Tailor's chalk

1 Begin making tabs by folding 3 in. (7.5 cm)-wide strip in half lengthwise, right sides facing. Sew long edges of strip together. Trim seam to ¼ in. (5 mm).

2 Attach a safety pin through both layers of fabric at one end of seam allowance. Push pin through opening of fabric tube and work it through to other end; pull pin and fabric to turn tube right side out.

3 Press fabric tube flat, centering seam along back of tube. Cut tube into eleven tabs, each 4 in. (10 cm) long. Adjust total number of tabs for curtains cut in any other width. Fold each tab in half crosswise with seam inside. Pin raw edges together.

4 Fold under and press 1 in. (2.5 cm) along each side edge of curtain panel, then fold under and press 1 in. (2.5 cm) again. Topstitch each side hem in place, then refold bottom hem and sew it in place.

5 Pin a tab at each upper corner of curtain panel, raw edges even and right sides facing. Pin remaining tabs along top edge of panel, spacing them evenly between both end tabs.

6 With right sides facing, pin unfolded edge of 2 in. (5 cm)-wide fabric strip to top of curtain panel, sandwiching tabs between panel and 2 in. (5 cm)-strip. The strip extends ½ in. (1 cm) beyond panel at each end.

7 Sew heading strip to top of curtain panel, catching ends of tabs in seam. Press seam toward curtain, and press under ½ in. (1 cm) extensions at each end of strip.

8 Fold heading strip to wrong side of curtain; press, then topstitch folded bottom edge in place.

TRY THIS!

When sewing fabric strips for the tab bows, make two extra strips to embellish the matching tiebacks. Make a buttonhole at the center of one end of each tieback. Sew a button to the opposite end. Make a buttonhole in the center of each bow strip. Button each strip to a tieback, then tie a bow to match the bows on the rod.

Making Bows for Tabs

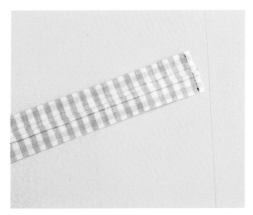

1 Cut eleven 3 x 20 in. (7.5 x 50 cm) strips of fabric. Fold each strip in half lengthwise, right sides facing. Sew long edges together, leaving an opening in center. Press seam open. Refold strip so seam runs along center, sew across short ends.

2 Trim seams, clip corners, and turn right side out through opening in seam. Press bow piece flat. Install curtain onto rod and tie bows around base of each tab top.

Crafter's Corner

Tab-top curtains call for decorative curtain rods, but these specialty items can be expensive. Consider adding purchased curtain rod tips, such as the cast-iron arrowhead and stylized iris design shown, to the ends of bamboo pieces. Or buy simple wooden knobs or finials and attach them to lengths of wooden closet poles. Paint, stain, or cover with paper or fabric as desired.

Look for interesting window treatments in home decorating magazines, catalogs, and stores, then search hardware and home stores to find ideal but inexpensive alternatives.

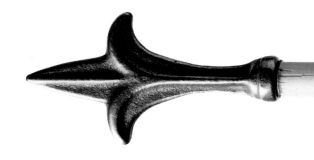

Decorating your curtain rods doesn't have to be expensive. Cast-iron arrowheads and stylized iris designs added to the ends of bamboo pieces make curtain rods interesting without being exorbitant.

Making Tabs from Trim

Fabric stores sell an incredible array of decorative trims that can be used in place of matching fabric tabs. Because their edges are finished, your job is even easier. Use trim about 1 in. (2.5 cm) wide. Consider adding tabs of eyelet or lace on sheer curtains; ribbon or braid will add pizzazz to solid-colored curtains. When working on lightweight fabrics, sew matching trim along the top of the curtain so that the edges of the tabs don't show through to the right side.

1 Fold under and press 1 in. (2.5 cm) twice along panel's side edges. Sew side hems of panel. Cut nine pieces of ribbon, each 4 in. (10 cm) long. Fold each in half and pin to wrong side of curtain, place a tab at each end and space remaining tabs evenly across.

2 Cut a piece of ribbon to fit across top of curtain with ½ in. (1 cm) extensions at each end. Pin edge of ribbon along seam with wrong side of ribbon overlapping seam allowance and sandwiching ends of ribbon tabs between.

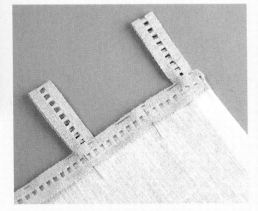

Linen fabrics are made from natural linen fibers and they range in weight from light, silklike textures to heavier grades with coarse textures. They are available in a wide range of colors, but look best in natural shades. Linen works with almost any decor and can be dressed up or down with trims. This linen curtain's soft look is accentuated by a simple tieback of braided jute with a decorative tassel.

3 Fold long ribbon over to right side of curtain, tucking under ½ in. (1 cm)-extensions at each end. Press and pin ribbon in place. Sew ribbon along each edge, catching ends of tabs in stitching.

Decorative Tiebacks for Your Curtains

The soft shirring of ruffled tiebacks greatly enhances the appearance of simple curtains.

Shirring tapes, available in a variety of widths, are a no-fuss way to sew gathered and ruffled tiebacks. Just stitch the tape to the back side of the tieback, then pull the cords to make even and uniform gathers.

You can custom design your tieback to suit the style of your curtain arrangement, selecting either a matching or contrasting fabric. If your curtains are a check, stripe, or plaid, as shown above, sew the tiebacks from matching fabric cut on the bias to create some visual interest. Secure the ends of the tiebacks with hook-and-loop fastening tape.

Different gathering methods create the tiebacks shown. The gathers on the tieback at top are achieved with a fabric tie that is threaded through a center casing stitched along the main tieback piece. The bottom tieback is made by gathering the main tieback piece, then sewing fabric ties to ends of the main gathered tieback.

Spruce up your window treatment with gathered or ruffled tiebacks. For a more stylish look, hold the tiebacks around the curtain without ties. Just sew snaps or hook-and-loop fastening tape to the short ends. To keep the curtains open, attach plastic rings to the middle of each short edge, then hang the rings from cup hooks attached to the window molding.

General Guidelines

Make tiebacks 3–4 in. (7.5–10 cm) wide for floor-length or heavyweight curtains. Make tiebacks narrower for sheer or lightweight curtains.

- Wrap cloth tape measure around pulled-back curtain to determine length for tieback.
- Cut fabric for gathered tieback to desired width plus 1 in. (2.5 cm), and two times desired length plus 1 in. (2.5 cm) for seam allowances.

Guidelines for Ruffled Tiebacks

- Cut both ruffled tieback and tie piece to two times desired width plus 1 in. (2.5 cm), and two times desired length plus 1 in. (2.5 cm) for seam allowances.
- If desired, place saucer at ends of ties and trace around shape to round ends. Fold tie in half lengthwise, right sides together, and seam edges, leaving opening on one long edge for turning.
- Insert tie through tieback casing. To hang, tie ends into bow or knot and hang from cup hook at window molding.

Making a Gathered Tieback

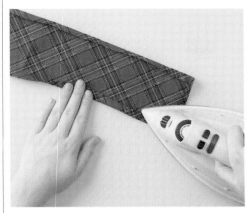

1 Following instructions in guidelines, cut fabric for 4 in. (10 cm)-wide gathered tieback. Press under ½ in. (1 cm) along all of the edges.

2 Cut 4 in. (10 cm)-wide gathering tape to length of fabric. Press ½ in. (1 cm) under at each end, pulling cords out to front. Pin to wrong side of fabric; edgestitch in place without stitching over cords.

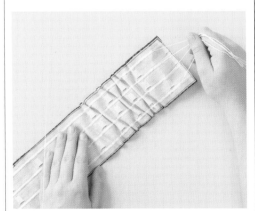

3 Knot cords at 1 end; pull evenly from other end, gathering tieback to desired length. Adjust gathers and knot cords in pairs. Leave ends long, so tape can be pulled flat for laundering. Attach fastener tape or snaps to short ends.

Making a Ruffled Tieback

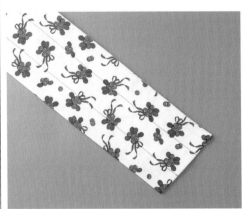

1 Cut fabric for 6 in. (15 cm)-wide ruffled tieback. Fold in half lengthwise, right sides together; seam long edges, leaving centered 2-in. (5-cm) opening on each short end. Turn right side out. Sew two parallel rows of gathering stitches 2 in. (5 cm) apart to form casing.

2 Cut 2 in. (5 cm)-wide tie. Turn tie right side out; press flat and slipstitch opening closed. Attach safety pin to one short end of tie and thread tie through casing.

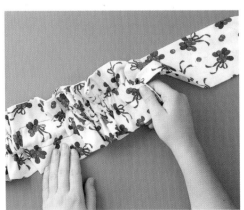

3 Pull tie ends to gather fabric. Make sure tie does not twist inside casing. Adjust gathers so they are even and tie ends are equal in length at both sides.

Curtains for Small Windows

Pretty hourglass curtains, softly gathered at the top and bottom edges, provide privacy and shade while giving a window a tailored, fitted look.

A double corded casing gathers each of these cheerful yellow-and-orange striped curtains at its center. Untie the cording and spread the panels for greater privacy. Since the treatment covers a large portion of the window, it is perfect for a room where little light is needed.

The hourglass design can be easily adapted to fit door or cabinet windows, and since hourglass panels can be hung from heavy-duty wires, they are an excellent solution for windows where it is impossible to install curtain rods.

For a simple alternative to casings, sew a pretty band with a sunny daisy on top to cinch in the sides of the panel. Or easiest of all, gather the fabric at the center with a pretty satin or velvet ribbon. Trim the ribbon ends diagonally for a nice finish and to prevent fraying.

Lightweight fabrics are the best choice for hourglass curtains, since they gather and hang evenly. Use sheer or lace fabrics for more light. Avoid loose weaves that may stretch after hanging.

General Guidelines

To use heavy-duty wire, install hooks on both sides of the window frame and make a loop at each end of the wire to slip over the hooks.

- For cutting length of fabric, measure length between rods; add 4 in. (10 cm) (twice heading allowance). For fabric width, measure length of rod, add 2 in. (5 cm) for side hems, then multiply by 2 or 2½. If fabric is sheer or lightweight, multiply finished width by three. Join fabric panels as needed.
- If placing two curtains in window: Divide width of rod in half; add 2 in. (5 cm) and multiply by two for cut width of each curtain panel.
- For casing, cut 2½ in. (6 cm)-wide strip to equal finished curtain width.
- To determine length of cinch band, wrap tape measure around gathered curtain; add 1½ in. (4 cm) for seams and overlap. Cut two 4½ in. (12 cm) -wide pieces to determined length. Sew two pieces together with ¼-in. (5-mm) seams; leave one short end open. Turn right side out; slipstitch opening closed and press.

You'll Need:
- ✓ Tape measure, scissors, straight pins, needle & thread
- ✓ Sewing machine
- ✓ Iron

For hourglass curtain:
- ✓ Striped fabric; cotton cording; two sash rods or heavy-duty wires & hooks
- ✓ Tailor's chalk

For cinch band:
- ✓ Blue & white fabric; yellow button; hook-and-loop fastener tape; paper

Sewing Hourglass Window Curtains

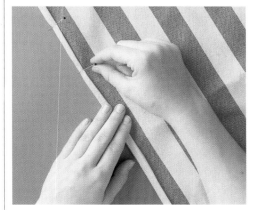

1 Install curtain rods or wires inside window frame about 1 in. (2.5 cm) from top and bottom edges. Follow guidelines to measure and cut fabric for curtain panels. Pin and stitch ½ in. (1 cm) doubled side hems.

2 At top edge, fold ½ in. (1 cm), then 1½ in. (4 cm) to wrong side; stitch. Stitch again ¾ in. (2 cm) from first stitching to form casing and heading above rod. Repeat for bottom edge. Fold curtain in half crosswise; press.

3 On casing strip, press under ½ in. (1 cm) on long edges; fold in half lengthwise; press, then open out. Pin to wrong side of curtain, with pressed lines aligned. Stitch long edges along pressed line.

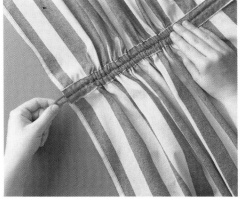

4 Thread length of cotton cord through bottom casing, then through top casing. Pull cord ends to gather fabric at center; knot cord. Hang curtain along top and bottom casings.

Sewing a Flower Cinch Band

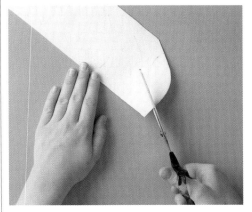

1 Make petal pattern 3½ in. (9 cm) long by 1 in. (2.5 cm) at widest. Trace and cut ten petals. Stitch petals with ¼ in. (5 mm) seam; leave 1 in. (2.5 cm) opening. Turn right side out; slipstitch opening closed; press.

2 Make blue band. Pin petals to center of band. From back, baste each petal ½ in. (1 cm) from center. Sew center down on front of flower, then attach yellow button to center. Sew fastener tape to ends of band.

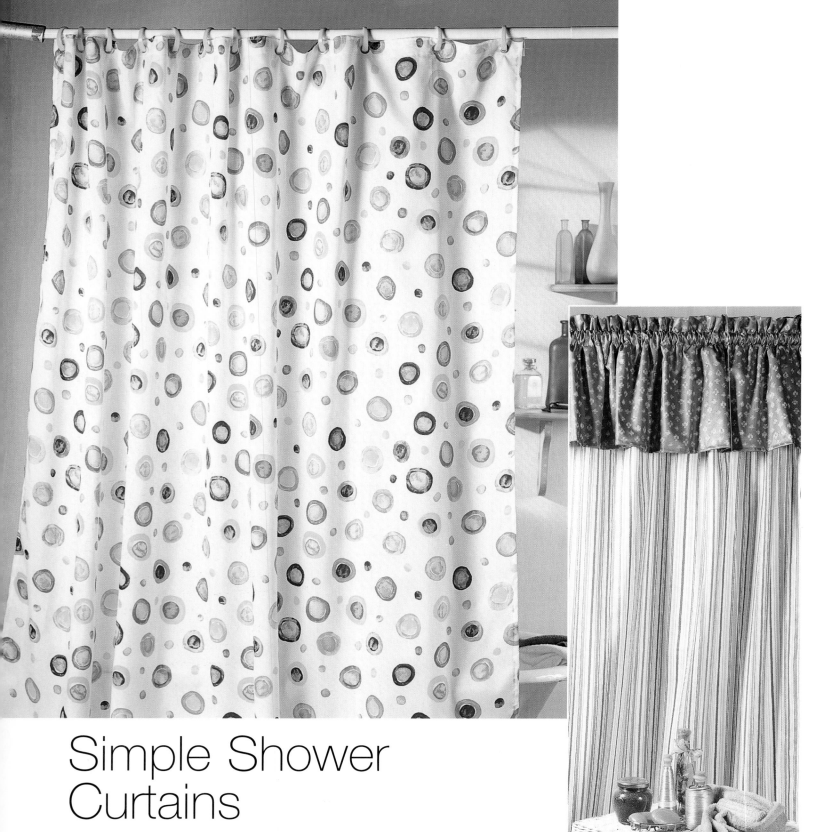

Simple Shower Curtains

Easy topstitching and purchased grommets turn the fabric of your choice into a custom-made shower curtain.

Often it is quicker and less tiring to make a simple shower curtain from decorative fabric than to shop around looking for a ready-made shower curtain that complements your existing bathroom tiles and fixtures. It's likely to be much less expensive too.

After finding the perfect fabric, sew panels together and install metal grommets to create sturdy holes for the matching curtain rings and to give the curtain a professional finish. Then purchase a plastic liner and hang it behind your brand-new shower curtain.

To give your shower curtain a softer, more appealing look, make a 16 in. (40 cm) long valance from coordinating fabric. Stitch a rod pocket and heading along the top edge and hang the valance from a separate rod.

A shower curtain can be made from any 45 in. (1.14 m)-wide washable fabric used to make window curtains. Avoid very delicate fabrics that can be damaged by moisture. You can also make the shower curtain from waterproof material, such as plastic sheeting, and eliminate the need for a separate plastic liner.

General Guidelines

The shower curtain will require piecing to obtain the proper width. For a standard 72 x 72 in. (1.83 x 1.83 m) curtain, cut and/or piece fabric to buy a 74½ in`. (1.89 m)-wide by 75¼ in. (1.92 m)-long panel of fabric. If the fabric has a large repeat pattern, buy extra yardage to match the pattern.

- Wash to preshrink fabric before cutting. Straighten grain.
- For odd-size shower curtain, measure shower rod, add 1¼ in. (3 cm) for each side hem, and allow extra half width for curtain fullness. For length, measure from curtain rod to at least 8 in. (20 cm) inside bathtub or almost to floor; add 3¾ in. (9.5 cm) for top and bottom hems.
- If piecing two panels, cut one panel in half along the length; sew each half to either side of full panel, using French seams.
- Follow manufacturer's instructions for installing grommets.

You'll Need:

✓ 4½ yd. (4.1 m) of 45 in. (114 cm)-wide fabric & matching thread

✓ Tape measure, pins, sewing machine, & iron

✓ Scissors & fabric marking pen

✓ Grommets, grommet tool, & hammer; seam sealant (optional)

✓ Shower curtain rings & plastic liner

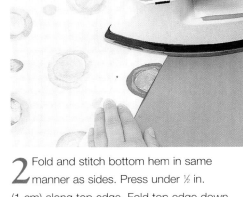

1 Cut and piece fabric so panel is 74½ in. (1.89 m) wide and 75¾ in. (1.92 m) long. Fold under and press ½ in. (1 cm) along each side edge; fold under and pin ¾ in. (2 cm) to wrong side; press. Stitch close to inner fold.

2 Fold and stitch bottom hem in same manner as sides. Press under ½ in. (1 cm) along top edge. Fold top edge down 2 in. (5 cm) for hem. Pin in place; press.

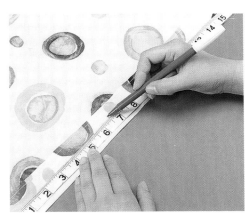

3 Stitch close to inner fold. If using plastic sheeting, no hemming is needed. If using laminated or waterproof fabric, do not pin, which leaves holes; stitch carefully, as removing stitches will leave holes.

4 Using a marking pen, mark grommet placement about 1 in. (2.5 cm) from top edge, beginning ¾ in. (2 cm) from each side, and about 6 in. (15 cm) apart. If liner is being used, align with top of shower curtain and mark through liner ring holes.

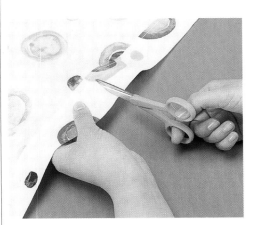
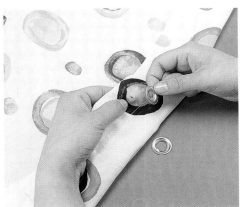

5 With sharp scissors, cut scant ½ in. (1 cm) vertical slit at each marking through all fabric layers. (Some grommet kits include a hole puncher.) If slit frays, spray seam sealant over threads to prevent further unraveling.

6 Once all markings are cut, insert front grommet section through slit so shaft extends to wrong side of curtain.

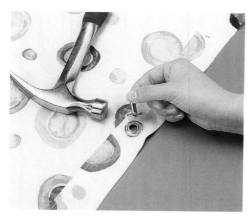

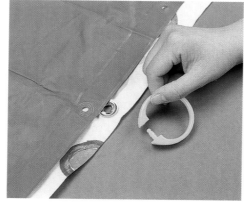

7 Lay curtain wrong side up on protected surface. Place grommet back over grommet front. Insert grommet tool in center of grommet. Hammer tool so front shaft flattens and folds over grommet back.

8 Repeat grommet insertion in all remaining openings. Lay liner over wrong side of curtain so holes align. Slip curtain rings through holes in both curtain and liner and hang from curtain rod.

Crafter's Corner

For a super quick shower curtain, use a flat sheet. There's no piecing and the hems are already made, although you will have to cut the length and remake the bottom hem. A flat twin sheet is generally 66 in. (1.67 m) wide, which will result in fewer gathers than a standard 72 in. (1.82 m) wide shower curtain; a flat full sheet is about 81 in. (2 m) wide, giving a bit more body.

TRY THIS!

Use artist's acrylic paints and a paintbrush to transform a clear plastic shower curtain into an exciting, custom creation. Lay the curtain out flat on the floor. Starting at the bottom, paint large geometric shapes—circles, squares, diamonds, triangles—in vibrant primary colors on the outside of the curtain. Make the shapes progressively smaller as you proceed up the shower curtain. Use a cardboard template to trace the shape outlines, or use masking tape to mark the straight-sided shapes, then paint inside taped lines. Let the paint dry thoroughly.

Appliquéing a Fabric Curtain

Make or purchase a solid-color fabric shower curtain and decorate it with fabric appliqués to create an original design. Closely woven fabrics printed with clearly defined motifs are easiest to use.

To avoid laundering problems, choose an appliqué fabric with the same care requirements as the shower curtain. Paperbacked fusible web makes it easy to apply the fabric motifs to the fabric curtain and the adhesive in the web helps prevent motif threads from raveling.

Coordinate your decorating efforts by using the same appliqué print fabric to edge towels and make curtains and other bathroom accessories.

Fabric appliqués look especially dramatic on the large expanse of a plain fabric shower curtain. Cut as many motifs as desired to fill the curtain with pattern and design.

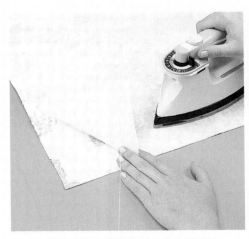

1 Iron shower curtain to remove wrinkles. Following manufacturer's instructions, iron paperbacked fusible web to back of uncut appliqué fabric.

2 Using small, sharp scissors, carefully cut out a selection of different patterns and different-size motifs from appliqué fabric.

3 Lay shower curtain on large flat surface, such as floor. Position motifs on curtain, moving them around for most attractive arrangement. Remove paper backing and pin motifs in place. Fuse motifs one at a time.

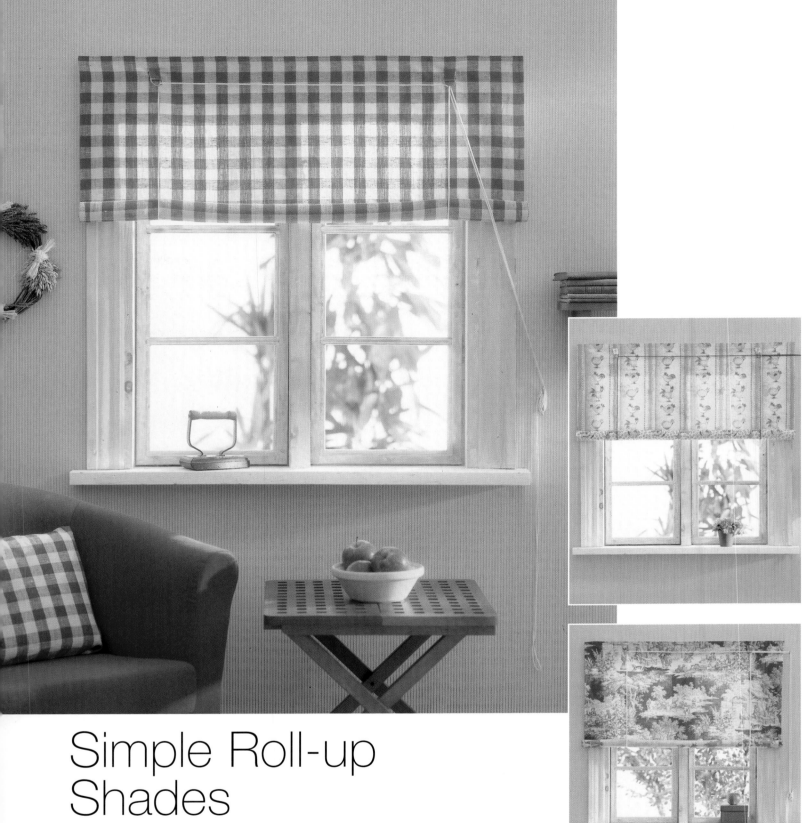

Simple Roll-up Shades

A centuries-old style of window covering, a fabric roll-up shade is appealing for its simplicity of design and ease of handling.

The shade is operated by an ingeniously, simple system of cords and rings that rolls the fabric up from the bottom. A dowel sewn to the bottom of the fabric helps the shade hang well and roll up evenly.

Roll-up shades require little fabric and sewing, and install easily. The simple roll-up design is well suited to casual prints like this red-and-white check.

For a custom look, coordinate the shade with throw pillows or other room accents. If desired, combine the shades with curtains and valances for a more polished treatment.

If desired, fuse a coordinated print to the shade back, as was done with the whimsical hen print. Add a pull cord in a contrasting color and extend it to the wall for a play of color and patterns when the shade is raised. Use a formal tapestry-like print to glamorize an austere room.

Make the shade from a single fabric panel, if possible, to avoid seaming. Densely woven medium-to heavy-weight fabrics work best. Lightweight fabrics must be lined to hang smoothly.

Guidelines for Measuring Fabric

Install the curtain rod before measuring for fabric.

- For shade width, measure curtain rod from end to end and add 1 in. (2.5 cm) for each side hem and ½ in. (1 cm) for joining seams, if needed.
- For shade length, measure from top of rod to windowsill; add 3 in. (7.5 cm) for pole casing and top hem.

Guidelines for Pull-up System

Install the pull up cord with the shade fully lowered.

- Attach awning cleat to side of window frame or to wall beside window.
- Sew one end of cord under hook-and-loop tape on back left side of shade. Hang shade. Thread cord around dowel in shade bottom, up through left ring, over through right ring, then out and down around awning cleat; double cord back through right ring, around bottom of shade, and back up to hook-and-loop tape at back right side; stitch cord end.
- Adjust cords with shade lowered so tension on both cords is equal.

You'll Need:

- ✓ Decorator fabric
- ✓ ⅛-in. (3-mm) cord (amount depends on length & width of shade)
- ✓ ¾ in. (2-cm) wooden dowel, cut to shade width
- ✓ 1 in. (2.5 cm)-wide self-adhesive hook-and-loop tape
- ✓ Flat sash curtain rod
- ✓ Awning cleat & two metal D-rings
- ✓ Scissors
- ✓ Sewing machine & thread

1 Follow guidelines to measure and cut fabric. Stitch ½ in. (1 cm) double hems along both sides; press. Fold top edge over ½ in. (1 cm), then pin loop side of fastener tape along folded edge.

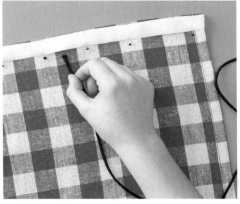

2 Cut length of cord equal to 6 times shade length plus shade width. Pin one cord end under fastener tape, 6 in. (15 cm) from left edge of shade. Stitch along top and bottom edges of fastener tape, securing cord in place.

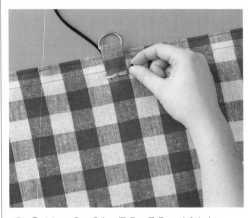

3 Cut two 3 x 3 in. (7.5 x 7.5 cm) fabric pieces for loops. Fold each in half, right sides together, stitch long edge; turn right side out. Thread loop through each D-ring; stitch loops, rings up, to shade front, about 6 in. (15 cm) from each side and just below tape.

4 Trim seam allowance of each loop if necessary. Fold loops down so rings face downward. Stitch second seam along folded edge to secure loops in place.

5 Double-fold bottom edge of fabric toward wrong side, first ½ in. (1 cm), then 2 in. (5 cm); pin. Stitch folded edge to make casing for dowel. Insert dowel into casing.

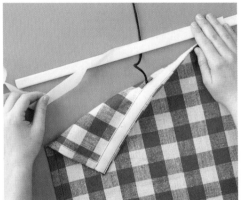

6 Attach hook side of fastener tape along front of curtain rod. Press tape edge of shade along rod. Assemble pull-up system as described in guidelines. Handstitch remaining cord end behind fastener tape on back right side of the shade.

TRY THIS!

If you'd rather not have any hardware showing, thread the cord directly through the fabric loops. Sew the loops as described on page 45, leaving out the metal rings.

To avoid bulky hems on the sides of the shade, stitch over the raw edges using a wide, closely spaced zigzag or overlock stitch. Refer to your sewing machine manual for specific instructions. Keep in mind that you will not need to add any side seam allowances. You can also use the full fabric width to make the shade and leave the selvages as the finished edges. If you want to make a lining, bond the edges of the two fabrics together with fusible web.

Making a Paneled Shade

By combining identical prints in different colors, like these red, blue, and green stripes, you can sew a roll-up shade that is bursting with colorful panache. The shade is hung and the cord system installed in the same manner as the main project except that the cord extends straight out to a hook at the side of the window.

Measure for fabric width as described in the guidelines for the featured project. To measure for length, measure the window height, and add 3 in. (7.5 cm) for top hem and bottom casing. Divide this total by three and add 2 in. (5 cm) for top and bottom seam allowances. Cut out three equal-sized panels from the different fabrics.

The loops for the pull cord are sewn in the same manner as for the featured shade, but instead of sewing rings into the loops, grommets are installed. The pull cord is kept neatly tied to the awning cleat by a hook screwed into the wall directly above it and in line with the grommets.

Rolled down, the three-paneled, tri-colored shade looks striking. It even looks interesting rolled up, showing only one or two of the fabrics. Three fabrics with the same pattern but in different colors create the most unified look.

1 Place top and middle fabric panels right sides together, with bottom edge of top fabric panel extending ½ in. (1 cm) beyond top edge of middle panel and side edges aligned; pin in place. Sew panels together with ½ in. (1 cm) seam.

2 Open out fabrics. Press seam allowances toward middle. Fold ½ in. (1 cm)-wide top seam allowance over smaller one; pin flat. Edgestitch along folded edge. Repeat to seam top edge of lower panel to middle panel.

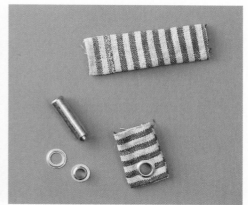

3 Make loops, then follow manufacturer's guidelines to install grommets; sew loops to shade. Hem side edges and make pole casing. Thread pole through casing at bottom of shade. Use hook-and-loop tape to fasten shade to rod.

Easy Roller Shades

With their clean, classic lines, fabric roller blinds offer discreet as well as informal elegance. They are also one of the easiest window treatments to sew.

Roller shades create subdued sophistication, and when coupled with other window treatments, they tend to fade into the background, allowing the more prominent treatments to take the center stage.

Making a fabric roller shade is not as tricky, or as costly, as it seems. Surprisingly, only basic sewing skills, a minimal amount of even-weave fabric, and scraps of fancy trims are all you need to create a treatment as attractive as the Victorian linen-and-lace blind shown here.

Sewing fancy borders across the bottom of roller blinds is an ideal way to flaunt your creativity. For a simple scallop finish, evenly space semicircles along the border edge and stitch to the bottom of the blind. Points also make an easy border, and both designs can be outlined with decorative upholstery trim.

Roller-shade kits are usually sold in home-decorating and fabric stores. Look for a cardboard or metal roller that will adjust to fit the size of your window. For a wooden roller, have the roller cut to size; just be sure to cut the end with the removable pin instead of the end with the permanent spring mechanism. Or reuse the roller from an old shade.

Sewing Guidelines

Tightly woven, medium-weight cotton fabrics work best for making shades. If possible, select a fabric that is attractive on both sides so the shade will look good when viewed from inside or outside of window. To avoid a seam down the length of your shade, use a fabric that is wider than the shade width.

- To determine shade width, mount brackets as desired to window frame, then measure distance between outside edge of brackets.
- To determine length, measure length of window, from top of brackets to bottom windowsill.
- When cutting out shade fabric, cut directly on vertical and horizontal grain lines.
- For casing that holds bottom slat of blind, cut 3 in. (7.5 cm)-wide strip of fabric with length to equal cut fabric width, plus 1 in. (2.5 cm). Stiffen casing fabric with starch.
- Treat unfinished edges of shade with fabric glue or liquid fray preventer.

You'll Need:

✓ Even-weave fabric
✓ Adjustable roller-shade kit
✓ Coordinating lace
✓ Matching thread
✓ Fabric glue or liquid fray preventer
✓ Pins & needle
✓ Tape measure
✓ Sewing machine
✓ Decorative tassel
✓ Brackets

1 Fold both short edges of casing strip under ½ in. (1 cm) and press. With right sides of strip facing wrong side of fabric and raw edges even, pin casing strip to one short edge of cut shade fabric.

2 Using ½-in. (1-cm) seam allowance, stitch as pinned. Turn strip to right side of shade and press flat. Fold top edge of strip under ½ in. (1 cm), then pin to form casing. Topstitch ¼ in. (5 mm) from folded edge of casing.

3 Measure and cut length of lace same width as bottom edge of shade. Lap lace edge over casing edge on right side of blind with all sides even. Topstitch lace in place, ¼ in. (5 mm) from edge.

4 To finish raw edges of shade, apply generous bead of fabric glue or liquid fray preventer to unfinished side edges of fabric and lace. Spread glue along fabric with fingertip, then let dry.

5 Position roller on right side of fabric along top edge. Remove backing from adhesive strip on roller, then secure fabric to strip. For wooden rollers, attach fabric with staple gun. Roll fabric tightly and evenly around roller.

6 With needle and matching thread, stitch purchased or handmade tassel to bottom edge of shade on wrong side. Slip slat into casing, then install shade in mounted brackets on window.

Sewing a Pointed Border

1 Cut two fabric pieces to same width as shade by desired depth, plus 1 in. (2.5 cm). Mark desired shape along one long edge; cut out. Right sides together, stitch along sides and shaped edge; turn and press. Stitch trim along shaped border edge.

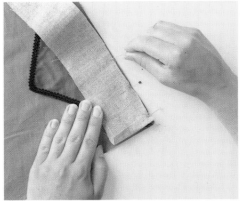

2 Wrong sides together and raw edges even, lay border over fabric. Right sides together, lay casing strip over border; pin and stitch ½ in. (1 cm) from edge of shade. Grade seam, then turn casing to right side; press. Finish shade as instructed.

Crafter's Corner

To check the grain of a woven fabric, pull a thread along each side of the fabric to mark the finished blind width. Pull a thread along the top and bottom edge of the fabric to mark the finished length. The measurement between the top and bottom threads on each side should be equal. Cut along pulled threads. As an alternative, use a dressmaker's pencil and T-square or yardstick to mark the measurements of the shade.

TRY THIS!

Creative borders change the look of a simple roller shade. To sew a notched border, cut a 6 in. (15 cm)-deep strip and stitch it to the shade as previously instructed for a casing. Form slat casing by topstitching 1 in. (2.5 cm) from the stitched top of the border. Draw a notch to the desired size in the center of the border so top of notch begins ¼ in. (5 mm) from the bottom of the slat casing. Cut out the notch, then finish raw edges with fabric glue or liquid fray preventer. For the dowel casing, topstitch ¾ in. (2 cm) from the stitched bottom edge. Insert the slat and dowel into their casings.

While borders add a decorative touch to roller shades, the shades themselves add a decorative touch to a room. Coordinate fabrics for window treatments with other elements in the room, such as slipcovers and pillows. Leftover pieces of upholstery fabric make beautiful matching shades.

Adding a Flounce to a Shade

A gathered piece of contrasting fabric adds a fanciful flounce to the bottom of a simple roller shade. When rolled up, the flounce becomes a soft valance.

Lightweight linen or cotton fabric is ideal for making the flounce. Complete the shade as previously indicated, finishing the raw edges with an overlock or hemstitch instead of fabric glue.

To make the flounce, cut two pieces of fabric at least 10 in. (25 cm) high, and the same width as the shade, plus 1 in. (2.5 cm). With right sides together and raw edges even, stitch one long edge and both short sides together with a ½ in. (1 cm) seam allowance. Turn right side out and press flat.

When choosing ribbon for the ties, look for a lattice-style ribbon with openings that can be used as buttonholes. Select buttons that will fit through the openings. If you prefer to use another type of ribbon, either make your own buttonholes or permanently stitch the ribbons in place on the front of the shade.

A gently curving flounce gives this floral blind the look of easy elegance. The soft white flounce is sewn to the shade just as any other decorative border, with pieces of ribbon added for tie-ups.

1 With raw edges even, lay flounce on right side of casing strip and wrong side of fabric shade over flounce. Position ribbons on sides between shade and flounce. Stitch through all layers, ½ in. (1 cm) from edge of blind.

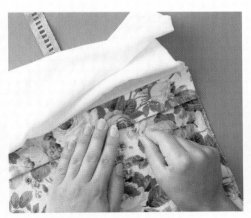

2 Fold casing to front of blind, then press casing, flounce, and ribbons flat. Turn casing raw edge under ½ in. (1 cm) and pin; edgestitch along top and bottom, ¼ in. (5 mm) from folded edges. Machine finish side edges or use liquid fray preventer.

3 Sew buttons to front of shade, with each positioned directly on top of each ribbon. Wrap ribbons around flounce, then slip over buttons to secure. Slip slat into casing, then install shade in mounted brackets.

Simple Throw Blankets

Who doesn't enjoy snuggling under a warm, cozy throw blanket? Since minimal sewing is required, you can quickly and easily make lovely blankets as gifts.

It is very easy and affordable to sew throw blankets for your own use or perhaps as housewarming, birthday, or holiday gifts. A crib or receiving blanket made of plush fabric makes a wonderful baby shower gift.

The blanket consists of a large piece of fabric that is bordered with attractive trim or decorative stitching. Depending upon the fabric and trim selected, the blanket can be customized to blend with any decor making it an ideal gift for any special occasion. This bright red-plaid blanket with snowy white fringe trim would make a perfect Christmas gift.

A coordinating pom-pom fringe on a printed throw blanket echoes the repeating motifs of an old-fashioned, Dutch-style patterned fabric. A blanket-stitched border accented with corner tassels gives this beige fleece throw a handsome, casual appeal.

Adding Wide Fabric Borders to a Throw

A nice alternative to finishing your blanket is to use two fabric layers and bring the bottom layer to the top to form a wide contrasting border. Select fabric for the bottom panel that coordinates in color or print with the top fabric.

Cut the bottom panel larger than the top panel so it can be folded to the front to make a border. For a finished 40 x 40 in. (1 x 1 m) blanket with a 2½ in. (6 cm)-wide border, cut a 36 x 36 in. (90 x 90 cm) top piece and a 46 x 46 in. (1.16 x 1.16 m) bottom piece.

With this border-forming technique, the corners of the bottom panel are stitched to form the mitered corners of the border before the top and bottom panels are joined. The bottom piece then acts like a frame under which the top panel is positioned.

1 Fold bottom panel in half diagonally, right sides facing. From point, measure 6 in. (15 cm) along unfolded edge and mark; draw right angle line from fold to mark; repeat on opposite corner. Refold on other diagonal and repeat.

2 Stitch along the marked line, stopping stitching about ½ in. (1 cm) from fabric edge. Trim fabric corner ½ in. (1 cm) from seam. Press seam open. Repeat for each corner. Turn corners right side out and press 3-in. (7.5-cm) border in place.

3 Press under ½ in. (1 cm) along inside edges of formed border. Lay top piece, right side up, over bottom and tuck raw edges under pressed border edges; pin in place. Edgestitch along pinned border edges.

To give the blanket a softly padded effect, use prequilted fabric or add a layer of polyester batting between the front and back panels and then anchor it in place with rows of machine quilting. Finish with a tassel in each corner.

Decorative Details for Pillows

Sew a pretty group of coordinated tie-on pillow covers in bright, harmonizing colors to liven up a mundane setting.

The ties can be made as wide and as long as you like, depending on whether you want to tie knots or bows and whether you want them to be discreet or noticeable. The ties and overlapping flap closure of the pillow cover can be made from the same fabric or from a contrasting one, such as in the red pillow above. To create a coordinating set, make each tie from the different fabrics used.

The pillow ties add a stylish and well-crafted look to any decor. They also make it easy to remove the pillow cover whenever necessary for laundering.

Sew a duo of big, soft coordinating tie-on pillows from different yet complementary fabrics. Make the ties for one pillow from the fabric of the other pillow. If the cover opening is on the side, sew the ties to one or both sides; if you prefer a center opening, fasten it with two pairs of ties.

For a pillow that will receive heavy use, select firmly woven, easy-care fabrics. Feel free to use more delicate fabrics if the pillow is meant to be purely decorative. Choose colors for the covers, ties, and closure flap that coordinate well with one another and with the colors of the room's decor.

This style of pillow covering looks best on a square pillow. Square pillow forms can be purchased at sewing centers and fabric and upholstery stores.

General Guidelines

Sew two or more ties along the pillow opening, as you prefer. For a standard 15-in. (38-cm) pillow, space the ties 5–6 in. (13–15 cm) apart and at an equal distance from the edges.

- For pillow-cover fabric, measure length and width across center of pillow. Cut two fabric pieces to pillow size plus ½ in. (1 cm) all around for seam allowances.
- For closure-lining flaps, cut two 7 in. (18 cm)-wide pieces of fabric equal to opening edge plus 1 in. (2.5 cm).
- Ties illustrated are 10 in. (25 cm) long and 1 in. (2.5 cm) wide. Adjust length and width of ties to suit size and style of bow or knot you plan to use. Cut ties to desired length plus 1 in. (2.5 cm) for seam allowance and two times desired width plus 1 in. (2.5 cm). Ties sewn from heavy fabrics will need to be made slightly longer in order to tie neatly. If you would like to have large bows, tie similar bow with tape measure to determine length.

You'll Need:

✓ Fabrics for pillow cover, closure flap, & ties
✓ Square pillow form
✓ Straight pins, hand-sewing needle, & thread
✓ Scissors & tape measure
✓ Sewing machine & iron

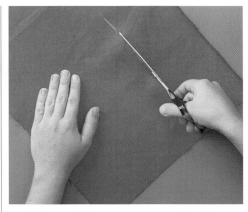

1 Follow guidelines to measure pillow form. From one fabric, cut two pieces for pillow cover and two pieces for closure flaps. Cut four ties from contrasting fabric.

2 Place fabric pieces for pillow cover together, right sides together and raw edges aligned. Stitch three sides with ½-in. (1-cm) seams, leaving one side open.

3 Fold each tie in half lengthwise, right sides together; seam, make sure to leave one end open. Turn right side out; press. Pin mark center of cover's opening edges. With raw edges up, pin two ties centered 6 in. (15 cm) apart on right side of each opening edge.

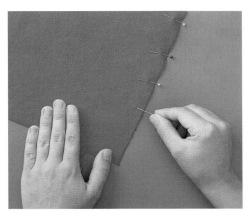

4 Place closure-flap pieces, right sides together and edges aligned. Pin short ends together. Sew along short ends with ½-in. (1-cm) seams to form ring; press seam open.

5 Turn closure-flap ring right side out. Slip flap ring into cover, right sides facing; with raw edges even and side seams aligned, pin flap to edges of cover. Stitch through all layers with ½-in. (1-cm) seam, securing ties in between.

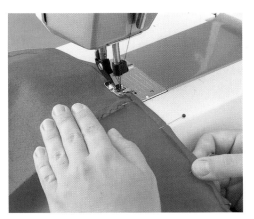

6 Open out closure flap from pillow cover and double-fold ¼-in. (5-mm) hem along remaining raw edge; pin and stitch. Fold closure flap over top side of cover, wrong sides together. Press seams flat.

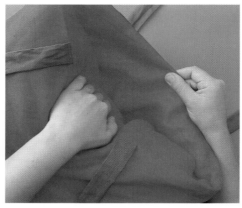

7 Leave pillow cover inside out. Using doubled thread, baste lower corner edge of closure flap to seam allowance of pillow cover. Repeat on other side.

8 Turn cover right side out and poke out corners to sharpen. Insert pillow form into cover; slip pillow end under one side of closure flap to hide. Smooth edges of opening.

9 Adjust cover so it lays smoothly and evenly over entire pillow form and fabric does not pull when opening is closed. Close cover by making decorative knots or bows with ties.

Crafter's Corner

Instead of making the ties yourself, use purchased ribbon. There are many colors and styles of ribbons to choose from, so you should have no problem finding ribbons that complement your pillow-cover fabric. Consider adding texture to the pillow covers with velvet, jacquard, embroidered, or woven ribbons. Whatever ribbon you choose, cut the ends at an angle to help avoid fraying and to give a neat finish.

TRY THIS!

Pillow ties don't always have to be practical; sometimes they can be purely decorative. Here, a single broad pair of ties are sewn into the side seams and then tied in large pretty knots on the front of the pillow. The ties of a fabric that matches but contrasts with the pillow cover can be knotted in the center and basted down as a bow, or tied once near the top of the pillow and basted down to form a twisted bow.

Knotting Pillow Corners

For variation, make a casual pillow that is knotted at each corner. The additional fabric for knotting is cut as part of the cover shape.

For a 16-in. (40-cm) square pillow, follow the grid below to make a pattern for the pillow cover with extended corners.

Fold a 33-in. (84-cm) square of pillow fabric into quarters. Pin the pattern to the fabric, aligning inner right-angle corner with the folded edges of the fabric. Mark the pattern, then cut out cover, adding ½-in. (1-cm) seam allowance. Cut out a second piece in the same manner.

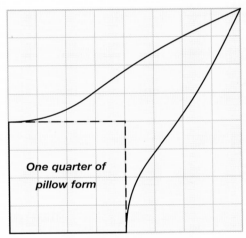

One quarter of pillow form

1 square = 2 in. (5 cm)

A covered square pillow with a large knot tied at each corner is informal and understated. Casual cottons or other relaxed fabrics are best suited for tying. Use fabrics with checks or stripes to create exciting patterns.

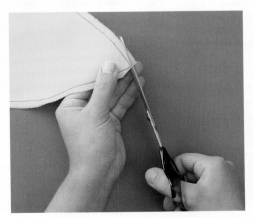

1 With right sides facing and edges aligned, pin both fabric pieces together. Stitch with ½-in. (1-cm) seam, leaving large opening on one side. Trim diagonally across seam allowance at corners. Turn cover right side out.

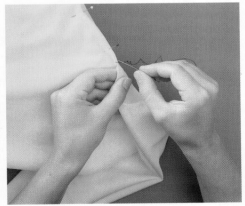

2 Insert pillow form in cover. Adjust cover so pillow is centered and corners are even. Slipstitch opening closed. If desired, sew zipper in opening following manufacturer's instructions.

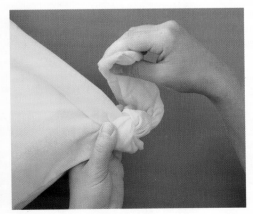

3 Smooth fabric over pillow, adjusting corners to even lengths. Gather fabric at each corner and tie in tight knot at edge of pillow. Tie second knot over first. Repeat for all corners.

Pillows with Romantic Ruffles

Toss on lots of light and airy ruffled throw pillows to add plushness and comfort to a chaise longue or a bed. Make the pillows from scratch or sew ruffled covers for ready-made forms.

Ruffles add interest to a pillow and can enhance needlework designs by acting as a frame for the handwork. Ruffled pillows made from embroidered fabrics and eyelet lace are a lovely addition to rooms with a romantic decor. In striking bold colors and prints, they blend into more contemporary settings.

Coordinate fabrics with curtains and spreads to tie the space together in an attractive, understated way. Make pillows square, round, or heart-shaped, whichever you prefer.

Sew on ribbons or a double ruffle, or make a patchwork front to give pillows more handcrafted details. Make many pillows and arrange them in an eye-catching group to create a soft, luxurious corner for lounging.

Pillow tops framed by ruffles make attractive showcases for embroidered eyelet fabrics. For a striking effect, use a colored fabric to make the pillow form.

Pillow-making Guidelines

Choose pretty fabrics that fit the design of the pillow, then embellish with rows of lace and bows if desired.

- Enlarge the diagram below onto graph paper and make two pattern pieces for heart-shaped pillow. Use half of heart shape for Pattern 1 and full pattern shape for Pattern 2.
- Use Pattern 1 to cut one pillow front and Pattern 2 to cut two pillow-back pieces.
- Use purchased ruffle or make enough ruffle to encircle pillow.

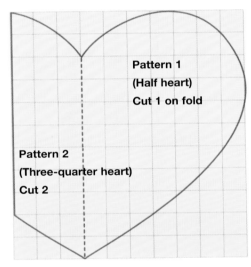

Pattern 1
(Half heart)
Cut 1 on fold

Pattern 2
(Three-quarter heart)
Cut 2

1 square = 1 in. (2.5 cm)

You'll Need:

✓ 1 yd. (90 cm) fabric for both pillowcase & pillow form
✓ Purchased ruffle trim
✓ Polyester filling
✓ Hand-sewing needle & pins
✓ Sewing machine & thread
✓ Tape measure
✓ Scissors
✓ Pencil & graph paper

1 Fold pillowcase fabric in half, right sides together. Place Pattern 1 on foldline for one pillow front and Pattern 2 beside it for two pillow backs. Cut with ½-in. (1-cm) seam allowances all around.

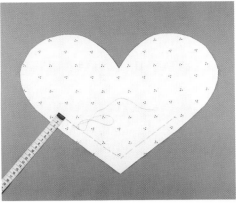

2 Hand-baste around pillow front 1 in. (2.5 cm) from edge, using contrasting-colored thread.

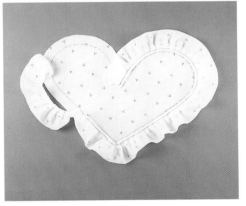

3 Place finished gathered edge of ruffle along basting line on right side of pillow front. Sew ruffle to pillow following ruffle's gathering line and overlapping ends to make seam look crisp and neat.

4 Turn under a ¼-in (5-mm) double hem along straight edge of pillow back; topstitch. Repeat with second back piece.

5 Right sides facing up, align back pieces to form heart shape, overlapping about 3 in. (7.5 cm) in center to create opening for inserting pillow form. Sew a seam along overlapping top and bottom edges of heart to hold firmly in place.

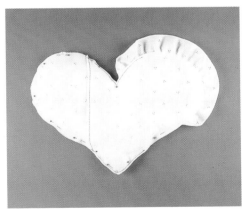

6 Right sides together, place pillow back on pillow front, matching edges and sandwiching ruffle in between. Pin, tucking ruffle inside to avoid catching it in seam. Topstitch around edge; clip at V.

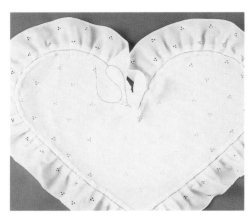

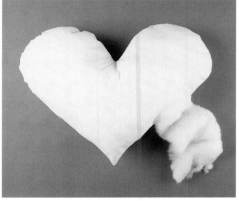

7 Turn right side out. Fold ruffle to back where two halves of heart meet and tuck under excess fabric. Hand sew along seam to hold excess fabric down; use small stitches to keep seam neat.

8 To make pillow form, cut two pillow front pieces with ½-in. (1-cm) seam allowances all around. Right sides facing, sew together along edge, leaving about 4-in. (10-cm) opening on one side of heart.

9 Turn right side out. Fill pillow with stuffing and slipstitch opening closed by hand. Insert pillow form into heart-shaped pillowcase.

Crafter's Corner

To make ruffles long enough to go around the pillowcase, measure very accurately. Ruffles are usually about 3 in. (7.5 cm) wide, but choose a larger or smaller width if desired. If you are using a ready-made ruffle trim, purchase a length equal to the pillow's perimeter plus 4–6 in. (10–15 cm).

If you are making ruffles, cut and join a length of fabric to equal twice the pillow's perimeter plus 4–6 in. (10–15 cm). Fold edges under ⅛ in. (3 mm) twice and hem. Make two rows of gathering stitches about ¼ in. (5 mm) apart along one long edge; pull thread ends to form uniform gathers.

TRY THIS!

Customize your pillows with pretty lace ribbons. Fabric stores have a large selection of fine lace yard goods and trims from which to choose. Select your favorite to create a pretty pillow to dream on or to use as a ring bearer's pillow at an upcoming wedding. For a truly romantic pillow, make a pillow front from cotton lace, then sew a double ruffle of lace onto the pillow front before sewing the front to the pillow back.

Making a Log Cabin Lace Pillow

Here is a pillow so appealing, with the inviting warmth of country patchwork and the softness of ruffles, that it is destined to become a family heirloom.

Use embroidered eyelet or combine different laces to piece the classic yet simple log cabin pattern, which evolves from a center square to which fabric strips are stitched, then cut to progressively longer lengths.

Plan ahead for the positions of special or favorite fabric scraps in the log cabin motif, such as a piece from a wedding dress or from a particular curtain or bedspread. Consider making a number of pillows with varied designs to create an exciting bed-top arrangement.

Wash and press all fabrics before sewing to avoid shrinkage when the pillow is washed. Press seams after each strip addition.

This pretty embroidered pillow, with its front pieced in a log cabin quilt pattern, has the look of an inherited keepsake. Because this technique is based on a very simple system of sewing strip to strip counterclockwise around a center square, it is not difficult to make.

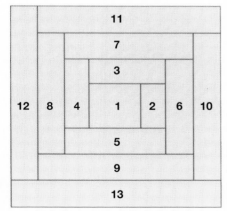

1 The log cabin pattern begins with a center square (1). A long fabric strip is stitched to the square, then cut to size (2); successive strips (3–13) are then stitched and cut to length in the numbered progression shown.

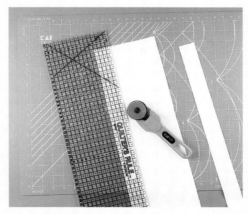

2 Cut out a 3-in. (7.5-cm) center square. Cut long 2 in. (5 cm)-wide strips of chosen fabrics to stitch and cut. For the neatest results, use a rotary cutter and cutting grid to cut strips accurately.

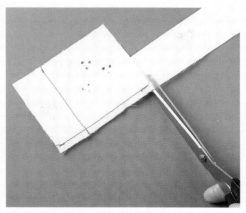

3 Right sides together, align and sew strip 2 to side of square. Cut off excess so strip and square are even. Turn counterclockwise; sew on strip 3; cut off excess. Continue adding strips until square is of desired size.

Decorative Pincushions

Beautiful pincushions are gifts any sewer will cherish. As practical as they are pretty, they keep pins safely collected and within easy reach.

Even sewers who only stitch hems and attach buttons need pincushions. Since these small beauties require a minimum of fabric and time, you can make enough to delight all your friends.

Select a rich brocade or tapestry to give the cushion extra body and style; or use wide embroidered ribbon to save time. Trim with gold cord and tassels for a rich look. Choose any of the shapes shown—either round, square, or pyramidal. Their wide bases will rest securely on a flat surface.

Pincushions can be made in a large variety of styles. Wrap fabric around fiberfill to make a soft cushion ball; tie a bow around the top, and use its ends to hold a thimble. Attach a velour-covered foam ball to a handy wristband. Glue a domed cushion to a box lid and store notions in the box. Cover any little odd container with wrapped fiberfill to make an unusual pincushion, like the miniature oval trough.

Make pincushion patterns in whatever sizes you prefer.

For best results, select a densely woven fabric, such as heavy cotton or tapestry, which can withstand multiple piercings by the pins.

Guidelines for Pyramid Cushion

Cut a square for the base. Cut four triangle pieces with one side to match the dimensions of the square and the other two sides slighly longer, to give the pyramid some height. Add ¼-in. (5-mm) seam allowance all around triangle pattern.

- If using fabric other than felt for base, add ¼ in. (5 mm) all around to fold under before attaching sides to base.
- To avoid hemming, use selvage of fabric or edge of ribbon as bottom of triangles.

Guidelines for Covering Box Lid

Boxes and foam balls are sold in craft stores; buy a ball with a diameter equal to that of the box cover.

- Using serrated knife, cut foam ball in half.
- Wrap velour around halved ball; mark outline of base with pencil on wrong side of fabric. Cut fabric, leaving ¼.–½ in. (5–10 mm) extra all around.

You'll Need:

✓ Scissors & pins

For pyramid cushion:

✓ Wide print ribbon; felt for base

✓ Stuffing or fiberfill

✓ Tassel & thin gold cording

✓ Pencil; tracing paper

✓ Sewing machine; needle & thread

For box-lid cushion:

✓ Round wooden box

✓ Foam ball

✓ Velour fabric; ribbon trim

✓ Craft glue

✓ Embroidery scissors; serrated knife

Making a Pyramid Cushion

1 Use triangle pattern to cut out four triangles from fabric or ribbon. Use square pattern to cut out felt for base.

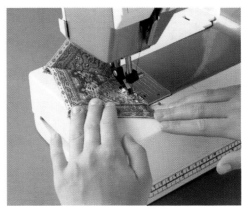

2 Place two triangles together, right sides facing; stitch ¼-in. (5-mm) seam along one edge, stopping stitching ⅜ in. (8 mm) below top point of fabric. Open fabric and repeat until all sides are sewn and pyramid is formed.

3 Insert end of tassel in small opening at top of pyramid. Handstitch tassel in place and slipstitch opening closed.

4 Center strips of thin gold cording over side seams of pyramid and slipstitch in place.

5 Place stuffing inside pyramid. To sharpen outline, use knitting needle, chopstick, or eraser end of pencil to push stuffing firmly into top point.

6 Tuck under the raw bottom edges of the pyramid. Pin square base to bottom of pyramid. Be sure corners are perfectly aligned. Slipstitch around all four sides.

Making a Box-Cover Pincushion

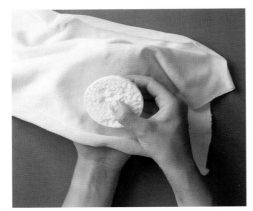

1 Wrap velour around top of halved ball to determine size of fabric circle; cut out circle. Apply glue along fabric edges; lay over rounded portion of ball, then wrap glued edges to bottom, clipping and overlapping edges so they lay flat.

2 Spread even layer of tacky craft glue over entire box cover. Glue velour-covered foam ball to box cover. Press down and hold together until glue sets and cushion is securely attached.

3 Glue decorative ribbon trim over seam between box cover and pincushion. Use pin to hold trim in place until glue is set.

TRY THIS!

Use your imagination to sew pincushions in a variety of interesting shapes such as these prickly cactus cushions. For a real cactus look, cut the pieces from green felt with pinking shears and sew the fronts and backs together with outside seams. Stuff each section before joining it to the rest of the cactus. Use the photos as guides.

Crafter's Corner

To give the pyramid-shaped pincushion better support, you can add a piece of cardboard to the felt base. Mark the square pattern on the cardboard, but cut out just a scant smaller all around. Either glue the cardboard to the wrong side of the base fabric or just hold it in place while you sew the base to the pincushion.

Sewing a Folded Pin Holder

For a nice alternative to a pincushion, sew a fabric "book" pin holder that folds up flat, its buttons closed, for compact storage and easy carrying. Place the closed pin book in a pocket or bag, and you're ready to go.

The protective cover of the pin holder is made from doubled decorative fabric; a piece of felt sewn inside holds the sharp pins. Cut the felt with pinking sheers for a decorative edge.

Select a densely woven cotton print to make an attractive cover and a small decorative button for a pretty closure. The button is sewn inside one short edge, and a buttonhole is sewn on the other edge. Make the buttonhole ⅛ in. (3 mm) longer than the diameter of the button. Use either your sewing machine's built-in buttonhole-stitch setting or its buttonhole attachment to make the buttonhole. Refer to your sewing machine manual for specific instructions.

A folded pin holder makes it easy to carry along pins and sewing needles, and it is also a practical and compact way of storing them. Make the cover from a fabric with a sewing-theme print, like these spools of whimsical threads.

1 Cut 18 x 5½ in. (46 x 14 cm) piece of fabric. Fold short ends to meet at center, right sides facing. Fold ½-in. (1-cm) seam allowance under on one short end, place seam allowance of other end over it, and pin. Pin and stitch long sides with ½ in. (1 cm) seam.

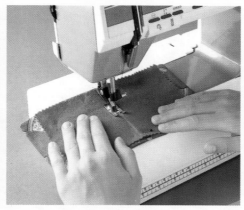

2 Turn cover right side out. With pinking shears, cut 7 x 4 in. (18 x 10 cm) piece of felt. Fold in half crosswise and use tailor's chalk to mark center. Place on inside of cover over middle joining, aligning centers; stitch along marking.

3 Machine stitch buttonhole at center of one short end. Hand sew button to center of inside cover on opposite short end. Fold cover in half and button pin holder closed.

Covering Tables the Easy Way

Brighten the look of your table with a striking circular tablecloth. In no time at all, you can stitch a table topper to suit any occasion.

Pretty fabric tablecloths are a very inexpensive and simple way to add color and pattern to your dining experience. Bold geometric colors are perfect for a fun and casual gathering; simple elegant stripes add classic appeal and are more appropriate for formal occasions. A quick change to a tablecloth made from a Christmas or Easter print adds a festive and fun touch for seasonal decorating.

With the large array of fabrics and trims available, the styles for circular tablecloths are limitless. Choose a tablecloth length that suits your table size and fabric.

A striped tablecloth turns an ordinary particle-board table into an intimate but eye-catching room accent. For a coordinated look, stitch napkins and place mats from fabric scraps left over from cutting out your tablecloth. Hem the edges as you would the tablecloth or embellish them with rickrack and other casual trims.

For best results, cut the tablecloth from washable fabrics that drape well and hang in loose folds. Avoid thin or stiff fabrics.

Tablecloth Guidelines

When sewing your circular tablecloth, use ½-in. (1 cm) seam allowances.

- To determine tablecloth diameter, add tabletop diameter to twice table height.
- If hemming edges instead of finishing with bias tape, add ½-in. (1 cm) hem allowance to tablecloth diameter.
- If fabric width is narrower than diameter of tablecloth, stitch panels together lengthwise before cutting out tablecloth.
- To determine yardage, multiply number of fabric panels needed by tablecloth diameter.
- Allow extra yardage when matching patterns, as ends of fabric panels may not be even after design is matched and may require trimming.
- For reversible finish, line tablecloth with contrasting fabric.
- Make circular place mats and coasters in same manner as tablecloth. Reinforce fabric by fusing lining fabric to back of place mats and coasters.

You'll Need:

✓ Fabric
✓ Matching thread
✓ Sewing machine
✓ Single-fold bias tape
✓ Tape measure
✓ Tailor's chalk
✓ Scissors & pins
✓ Iron

Matching Fabric Patterns

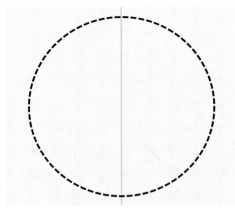

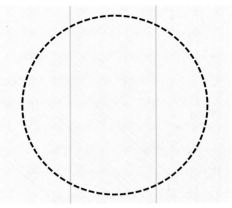

1 Stitch two fabric panels of equal size together to create large enough piece of fabric for tablecloth. Cut out circle with seam in center. This one-seam method is preferable when matching fabric pattern.

2 For full fabric panel along center of tablecloth, cut one panel in half lengthwise. Stitch each half-piece to each side of second panel. For extra-large tablecloth, stitch three full-size fabric panels together.

Joining Fabric Panels

1 To join two fabric panels, pin lengthwise edges together, right sides together and raw edges even, and stitch. Press seams open. If necessary, clip selvages to ensure seam lays flat.

2 To join patterned fabric, fold under seam allowance of one panel; press. With right sides facing up, position folded edge of panel over selvage edge of matching panel, aligning design; pin. Repin with right sides together and stitch together.

Sewing a Circular Tablecloth

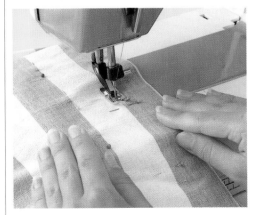

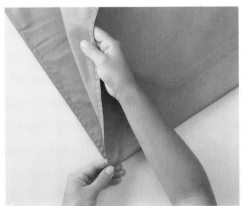

1 To join striped fabrics, align lengthwise, alternating stripes on panels; stitch along edge of one stripe line. When opened out, striped pattern should be continuous.

2 With wrong sides together and raw edges even, fold pieced fabric for tablecloth in half; then fold into quarters. Pin all raw edges together to prevent fabric from slipping.

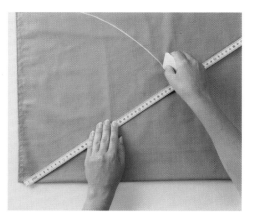
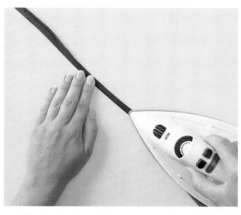
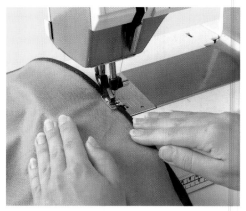

3 Position end of tape measure at folded corner and mark half of tablecloth diameter with tailor's chalk. Continue measuring and marking to form arc on fabric. Cut through all four fabric layers, using chalk line as guide.

4 Cut and piece bias tape together to make one continuous piece equal to tablecloth circumference (multiply cloth diameter by 3.14) `and then add 2 in. (5 cm). Fold and press bias tape in half lengthwise so that underside is ⅛ in. (3 mm) wider.

5 Enclose tablecloth edge with bias tape with wider side underneath. Topstitch bias tape to tablecloth, folding end of bias tape under and overlapping stitched end.

Crafter's Corner

A decorating idea that is both pretty and practical is to make a smaller topper to layer over a full-length tablecloth. Cut the topper from stain-resistant fabric, or fuse clear iron-on vinyl to the front of patterned fabric. Follow the basic instructions for making a circular tablecloth, but make the drop only 6–10 in. (15–25 cm) on all sides.

Unify the look by finishing both the topper and the tablecloth with matching binding. Or you can omit the binding by stitching the tablecloth front to a matching lining fabric, wrong sides facing and raw edges even. Leave an opening for turning. Clip curves and turn. Press seam flat and slipstitch opening closed.

TRY THIS!

Unusual hems change the look of your tablecloth. For example, a wide border sewn to the edge of a short tablecloth creates a charming café-style topper. To make, cut out tablecloth. Fold border fabric in quarters, aligning selvages. Fold tablecloth in quarters, then position on top of border fabric so folds are aligned. Mark edge of tablecloth onto fabric, remove tablecloth,

then mark again 1 in. (2.5 cm) toward center of fold. Mark outer edge of border 8½ in. (22 cm) from first marking line. Cut out border along marked lines. Right sides facing and raw edges even, stitch border around edge of tablecloth, clipping curves as needed; press. Topstitch along seam line. Turn raw edges of border under ¼ in. (5mm) twice and edgestitch in place.

Sewing a Bordered Tablecloth

An asymmetrical border is an ideal way to mix and match decorative fabrics. Choose two different colorations of the same fabric, like the tablecloth shown here, or fabrics that work well together. A floral print with a coordinating plaid, or a geometric with a solid border would also work very well. Add an interesting trim, such as rickrack, pom-pom trim, or a coordinating ribbon or textured braid.

To make the center, cut a square piece of fabric with a diagonal measurement equal to the diameter of the desired finished tablecloth; add ½ in. (1 cm) seam allowances all around. Cut four border pieces from a contrasting fabric, each width equal to one fourth the width of the cut square, plus 1 in. (2.5 cm), and the length equal to cut square edges. Stitch on the borders, then cut out the completed circle.

A round cloth sewn from two coordinating fabrics looks deceptively like two layered cloths instead of a single one. Complete the illusion by using fabrics in contrasting colors and finishing the edges with a different contrasting trim.

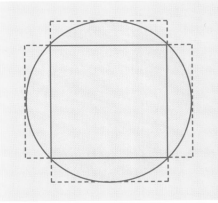

1 Making a bordered tablecloth is easier than it appears. Stitch fabric borders (dotted lines) to each side of square to create one large piece of fabric. Fold fabric into quarters, then draw and cut out the circular cloth.

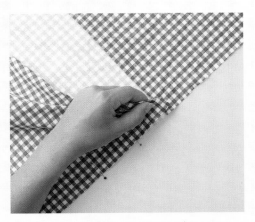

2 Wrong sides facing and raw edges even, stitch one border piece to each side of contrasting square. Press seams open. Fold stitched piece into quarters and mark circle as described in Step 3 on page 70. Cut out cloth.

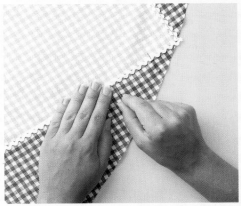

3 Lay tablecloth on flat surface. Pin and topstitch rickrack or other decorative trim along seams between contrasting fabrics. To complete cloth, finish edge of tablecloth with matching bias tape as before.

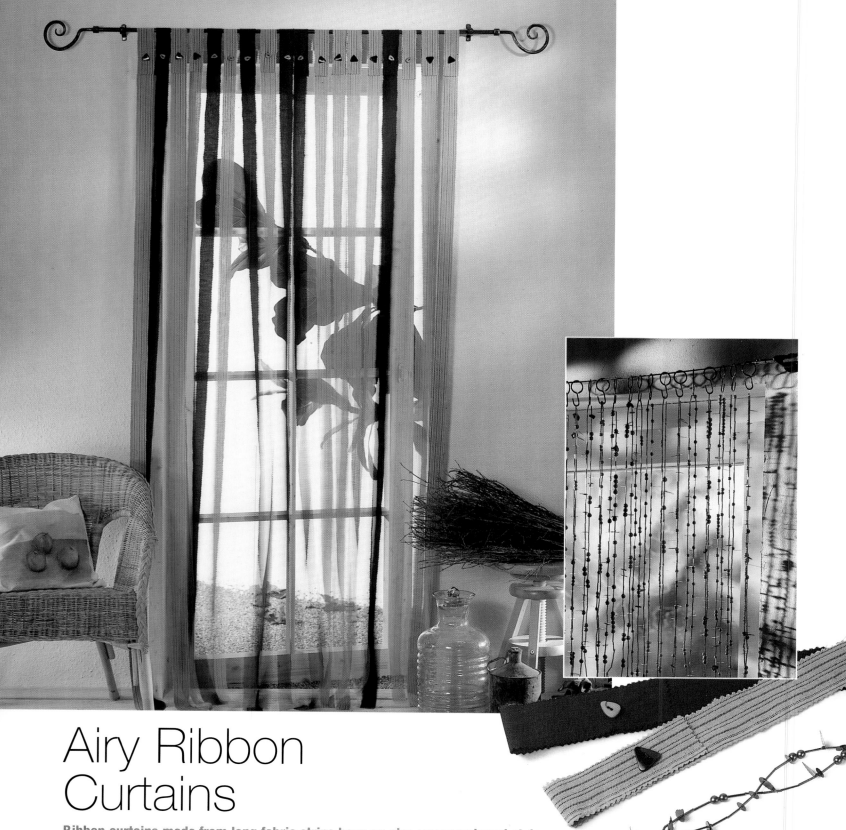

Airy Ribbon Curtains

Ribbon curtains made from long fabric strips have an airy, unencumbered style. With little cutting or sewing required, these free-floating window coverings can be finished in a flash.

Light and breezy ribbon curtains stylishly screen a window and make ideal door coverings and room dividers.

The ribbons are long strips of fabric torn along the lengthwise grain, then pinked. The top of each ribbon is folded into a loop for hanging on a pole and secured with a button.

Mixing and matching ribbon fabrics can set a room's tone, such as the seaside feel inspired by the blue and green fabrics.

Delicate curtains made from strands of similar colored beads convey a 1960s retro look. Combine thin and shaped beads for variety and interest. Contrasting tab-top ribbons sport decorative buttons in opposing colors.

Select a loosely woven decorator fabric in cotton, linen, or blends to make the ribbon curtains. A solid fabric or one with a pattern or stripe on the lengthwise grain can be used separately or mixed for interesting effects. Be sure the fabric looks good on both sides.

Beaded curtains are made simply by using a fine beading needle to string beads onto strands of nylon beading cord cut twice the height of the window or door. Note that you will need a large number of beads to cover an entire window or door. The largest selection can be found in bead stores or craft supply stores. Both of these places also sell beading cords and needles.

Ribbon Curtain Guidelines

An option to using fabric strips is to make the curtains from 2 in. (5 cm)-wide purchased cotton ribbon.

- Install curtain rod at desired height over window or door. Measure distance from rod to floor, add 5 in. (12.5 cm) for loop as well as for any floor-pooling desired.
- For number of ribbons needed, measure width of window or door and divide by ribbon width.

You'll Need:
✓ Tape measure
✓ Curtain rod or curtain wire

For ribbon curtains:
✓ Reversible fabric
✓ Scissors & pinking shears
✓ Decorative buttons
✓ Sewing needle & thread

For beaded curtain:
✓ Assorted beads
✓ Deep plate
✓ Beading needle
✓ Nylon beading cord
✓ Curtain hooks

Making a Ribbon Curtain

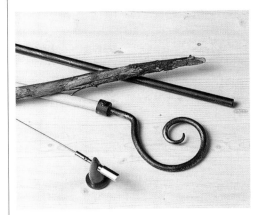

1 Select a metal, wood, or wire curtain rod to blend with your room decor. If desired, consider using natural materials, such as branches or rope.

2 Cut fabric to ribbon length; trim selvages. Along top edge of fabric, measure 2 in. (5 cm) -wide strips; clip top crosswise threads. Tear fabric strips along lengthwise grain.

3 Trim long, raw edges of torn fabric strips with pinking shears. Pink one short end on all strips.

4 Fold pinked short end over 5 in. (12.5 cm) to right side; pin. Measure 3 in. (7.5 cm) down from folded edge; mark center. Sew button through layers at mark. Repeat with remaining ribbons. Thread ribbons on rod; hang; pink bottoms to even length.

Making a Beaded Curtain

1 Place beads on plate or in bead tray. (Tiny beads can be collected on adhesive strip.) Cut nylon cord to double desired curtain length; knot one cord end. Use beading needle to thread beads; knot end.

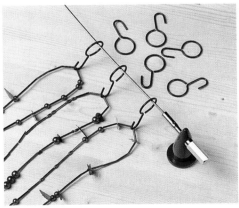

2 Attach curtain hooks to wire rod. Double beaded cord and drape over curtain hooks. Hang rod across window or door opening. Adjust spacing of hooks and even lengths of strung beads.

Fabric Panels

As stylish as it is practical, a fabric room divider serves as a soft door, separating rooms, providing privacy, and insulating areas from drafts and noises.

Easily constructed from two coordinating fabrics, the warm and inviting divider adds an extra dimension of color, pattern, and style to the rooms that it separates.

Select fabrics that complement the color schemes and decor of the rooms

they will be facing. This combination of bright yellow, green, and red floral and plaid fabrics suits a relaxed, informal setting. Held to one side by a ring sewn to the cover and slipped over a wall hook, the draped fabric creates a decorative pattern play.

A fabric room divider can be hung in many different ways, depending on your door opening and the style you prefer. As shown, you can hang sewn loops over hooks or thread ribbons through grommets and tie them around a curtain rod.

Install the hanging hardware before measuring your fabric. To use hooks, first install a mounting board above the doorway: Measure the doorway between the outer edges of the frame, then cut the mounting board 1–2 in. (2.5–5 cm) bigger on each side.

Fabric width equals the width of the mounting board or curtain rod plus 1 in. (2.5 cm) for seam allowances. For the length, measure from the floor to the hooks and subtract 2 in. (5 cm) for the tabs. Add 8½ in. (22 cm) for the bottom hem and the top seam. Cut one piece from each fabric.

Sewing Guidelines

Tabs are placed about 6½ in. (17 cm) apart; make as many as your width needs plus one extra to hold ring at side.

- For time-saving option, make hanging loops out of coordinating cotton ribbon. Ribbon must be sturdy enough to hold weight of fabric.

- To fold loops, lay them facedown on table. At middle, fold one half of ribbon so it is at right angle to the other half. Fold other half in the same manner, forming arrow shape. Stitch across top.

You'll Need:

✓ Sewing machine & matching thread

✓ Scissors, tape measure, & straight pins

For divider with tabs:

✓ 2 coordinating fabrics

✓ Thin matching ribbon

✓ 8 metal hooks

✓ Metal ring

✓ Iron

For sheet divider with grommets:

✓ Sheet

✓ Cotton ribbon

✓ Grommet tool & grommets

1 Follow guidelines to measure and cut out two fabric panels for divider. At bottom edge of both panels, press 4-in. (10-cm) double hem to wrong side of fabric; pin. Stitch along folded edge.

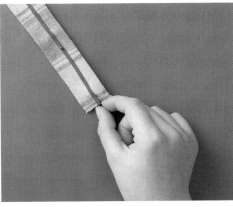

2 Cut 8 x 3 in. (20 x 7.5 cm) fabric strips for loops. Fold each strip in half lengthwise and seam long edge. Turn right side out and center seam on back; press. Pin and sew thin ribbon down center front of loop.

3 Set one fabric strip aside. Follow the guidelines to fold loops into pointed arrow shape. Pin loops on both sides, then stitch across top to hold folds in place.

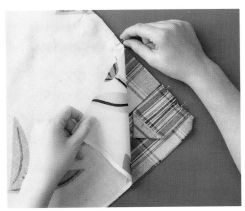

4 With one panel right side up, pin evenly spaced loops facedown along top edge of panel, raw edges even and points facing down. Lay second panel, right side down, over first panel; pin together along top edge, sandwiching loops.

5 Thread remaining loop through metal ring. Place loop between panels, about two-thirds of the way down on side edge, with raw edges even; pin. Stitch panels together along top and side edges with ½-in. (1-cm) seam.

6 Turn divider right side out and iron all seams flat. Pin thin ribbon in even line ½ in. (1 cm) below top edge. Stitch down center of ribbon to attach. Hang loops of divider on hooks over doorway.

Sewing a Sheet Room Divider with Grommets

1 Cut sheet to size needed, plus side and bottom hems and 4 in. (10 cm) for top hem. Sew 2-in. (5-cm) double hem at top. Install grommets at top side edges, then space remaining grommets evenly apart, about 3 in. (7.5 cm).

2 Cut 20 in. (50 cm)-long strip of cotton ribbon with diagonally cut ends for each grommet. Thread ribbon strip through each grommet. Knot ends, making small loops. Insert curtain rod through loops.

Crafter's Corner

You can follow the same simple method to quick sew an attractive panel to conceal storage shelves or an unattractive work area. Since the cover is seen only from one side, all you need is one fabric panel on which you double-fold ½-in. (1-cm) hems on the sides.

To divide a single room, hang a double-sided panel from hooks or a rod attached to the ceiling. The curtains are so easy to make you can change them seasonally or whenever you feel like updating your decor.

TRY THIS!

Hanging a heavy fabric panel in front of a door in winter is a beautiful way to keep the cold out of your home and the heat inside. Use it over a door to a sunroom or sunporch, an attic, or any drafty door that is not readily used in winter. Avoid using this type of fabric panel in high traffic areas, such as the front door. To make an easy insulating panel, use a duvet cover with a blanket as a liner. Following the fabric design, if possible, topstitch across the fabric to hold the blanket in place.

Insert grommets evenly along the upper edge, being sure to go through the blanket. Thread a length of extra sturdy ribbon through each grommet, and tie the ribbon into a loop. Or stitch two layers of regular ribbon together, then thread and tie into loops. Hang the panel from a pretty curtain rod installed above the door.

Covering a Bookcase in Fabric

Dressing a plain bookcase with pretty fabric panels is an ingenious way to keep it looking neat while adding color and style to a room. Made from two coordinating fabrics, the cover has easy open flaps so the contents of the shelves are always within reach.

The back, sides, and front of the cover are all cut from one length of fabric, so the cut fabric length equals the perimeter of the bookcase plus 1 in. (2.5 cm) for seams, less 4 in. (10 cm) for borders and the cut width of the cover equals the height of the bookcase plus 1½ in. (4 cm) for seam and the bottom hem.

Cut top piece from a contrasting fabric equal to the top measurement of the bookcase plus ½ in. (1 cm) all around. Also cut two 5 in. (13 cm)-wide border strips equal to the cut width of the fabric panel. Press each strip in half, lengthwise, wrong sides facing. Open out and press ½ in. (1 cm) under along one long edge of each strip. Cut four 1-yd. (90-cm) lengths of 2 in. (5 cm)-wide grosgrain ribbon for the ties.

A pretty fabric cover brings unexpected charm to an ordinary bookcase, while cleverly disguising shelves cluttered with toys and books. Pink ribbon ties let the curtains be drawn open for play time.

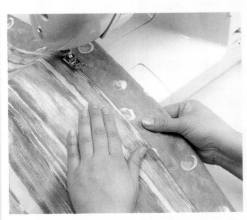

1 With raw edges even and right side of strip facing wrong side of main piece, stitch together. Press seam toward border. Refold strip, bringing pressed edge over seam line; edgestitch in place. Repeat for other border.

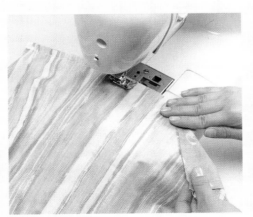

2 Sew ½-in. (1-cm) double hem along bottom long edge of panel. Notch center on long edge of top. Starting and ending at notch, pin panel to top, right sides facing; clip panel as needed to turn corners; sew.

3 Put cover on bookcase. Mark tie points halfway down and 1 in. (2.5 cm) in from each front corner. Remove cover. Fold ribbon end under; sew at marked point. Sew second ribbon at same point on wrong side. Repeat for other side.

Place Mat
Table Runners

Stylish runners are a welcome change from individual place mats, and they add color and style to your table setting while protecting your tablecloth from spills.

Layer the runners over a contrasting tablecloth or use them right on the table. Since only a little fabric is required, you can design runners in a wide range of different fabrics and styles to mix and match with other table accessories or to set a special table for a holiday meal.

The striped place-mat runners pictured combine handsomely with the blue-and-yellow floral tablecloth they protect. For a unifying touch, both the runner and the tablecloth are trimmed with the same thin blue ribbon.

Use different fabrics, edges, and finishing techniques to create runners in a wide variety of styles. A floral runner with scalloped edges and a pink bias-tape trim adds a feminine flourish to a pink-and-green-checkered tablecloth. A simple off-white runner with a geometric border has a more understated style.

Create a pattern for the shape of runner you want. Use a ruler for accuracy and a pair of compasses or suitable plate for curves, making sure your pattern is symmetrical.

The runners are made by sewing two layers of fabric together. Washable, stain-resistant fabrics are the best choice; for easy care, look for permanent press fabrics. Avoid thin or stiff fabrics.

Sewing Guidelines

The runner shown is 12 in. (30 cm) wide; however, you can make it wider if desired. To determine the length of your runner, measure the distance along the tabletop (either width or length) that the runner will cover, and add 8–12 in. (20–30 cm) for each drop. Add ½ in. (1 cm) for all seam allowances. Position and mark the contoured pattern along the short edges of the runner.

- To make corners sharp, trim straight across seam allowance at stitched point, then trim seam allowances at angle on either side of point.
- For added cushioning, use quilted fabrics or add thin layer of batting, lightweight interfacing, or fusible fleece between fabric layers.
- If desired, bind raw edges with bias tape in coordinating color. Cut tape length to equal perimeter of runner plus 4 in. (10 cm).

You'll Need:

✓ Fabric

✓ Scissors & straight pins

✓ Pencil & tracing paper

✓ Sewing machine & matching thread

✓ Iron

For pointed runner:

✓ Narrow matching ribbon

✓ 2 matching tassels

✓ Seam ripper

For scalloped runner:

✓ Single-fold bias tape

1 Fold fabric in half lengthwise, right sides facing. Trace around pointed pattern on doubled fabric layer; extend sides to desired length; mark pointed shape on opposite end. Cut out pieces.

2 Sew fabric pieces together, right sides facing and edges aligned, using ½-in. (1-cm) seam allowance. Leave 3-in. (7.5-cm) opening for turning along one long side.

3 Trim seam allowance at pointed ends. Turn right side out and press with warm iron. Fold edges of opening under ½ in. (1 cm); press flat. Slipstitch opening closed.

4 Leaving 2 in. (5 cm)-long tail, pin ribbon to one short end of runner, ¼ in. (5 mm) from edge. At center point of runner, knot ribbon and pin knot just above point. Continue pinning along other half of short end; leave 2-in. (5-cm) tail. Repeat at opposite end.

5 Using seam ripper, make small openings in seams at sides of runner. Poke ribbon ends through openings to hide ends. Topstitch along center of ribbon to secure it in place. If necessary, slipstitch opening closed. Repeat at opposite end.

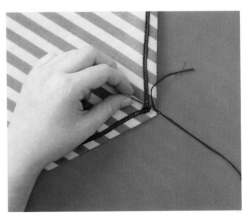

6 Thread long end of tassel through needle, then hand stitch tassel through knot at one point of runner. Repeat with remaining tassel at opposite end.

Making a Scalloped Runner with Bound Edges

Making a Geometric Runner

1 Press binding tape in half lengthwise with one half slightly wider than other half. Cut out runner with scalloped ends. Place pieces together, wrong sides facing. Baste edges if desired.

2 Pin binding over raw edges with narrow side of binding on top. Position pins tightly along curves. Turn under top end of binding where it overlaps beginning. Edgestitch binding in place.

Mark and cut out geometric runner. Stitch together front and back, right sides facing, leaving 3-in. (7.5-cm) opening. Clip into seam allowances at inside corners; trim seam allowances at outer corners. Turn right side out; press. Slipstitch opening closed.

TRY THIS!

Create a place-mat runner with a practical twist—handy napkin pockets sewn on both ends. Add an extra 5 in. (13 cm) to the length of a straight-edged runner for each napkin pocket. Stitch the panels together, right sides facing; turn right side out; and press. Then fold up the pockets and slipstitch in place; if you prefer, topstitch them along the side edges. Complete the look with coordinating napkins sewn to match your runner and tablecloth.

Crafter's Corner

If you want to make your runner wider to accommodate more elaborate place settings, you can use a ruler and pencil to mark a new pointed end. Cut the runner to the desired width plus a seam allowance on each side. Fold the fabric in half lengthwise and mark the center point along each end. Open the fabric and measure 3 in. (7.5 cm) up from the ends on both sides, then connect the markings to the center point.

Sewing a Ruffled Runner

Pretty ruffles lend softness and charm to a white eyelet runner. This runner was made from eyelet yardage and trimmed with a bordered eyelet ruffle.

Cut out two fabric panels, 12–14 in. (30–35 cm) wide, with straight edges at the ends; carefully match the eyelet patterns on both layers.

Make a pattern for the border ruffle. Place pattern tissue on the fabric panel. The width of the pattern should match the width of the runner, the height of the pattern should match the depth of your eyelet ruffle. Round off the two short ends of the pattern. Using the pattern, cut ruffle one and a half times pattern width for fullness. To gather the border with a sewing machine, loosen the top thread tension and make two rows of gathering stitches ½ in. (1 cm) and ¼ in. (0.5 mm) along straight end of ruffle, continuing out on to short ends of ruffle. Place ruffle on pattern guide and pull the bobbin threads to form gathers. Gather the ruffle until it matches the finished width of the runner, easing ends of the ruffle into rounded shape. Distribute gathers evenly, then secure them by wrapping the thread ends around pins inserted at both sides.

A soft and pretty white eyelet runner with lacy, ruffled ends lends a casual elegance to a romantic dinner for two. Lay the light, delicate-looking runner over a bare wood table to accentuate the natural beauty of the wood.

1 Place pattern on ruffle fabric with straight edge along finished eyelet border; cut out. Sew two rows of basting stitches along curved edge; pull bobbin threads to gather until ruffle is 1 in. (2.5 cm) shorter than unsewn width of runner.

2 Center ruffle, right sides facing and raw edges aligned, on each end of top runner piece; pin in place, beginning and ending ½ in. (1 cm) inside outer edges. Wrap ends of gathering threads around pins to secure. Stitch ruffles in place.

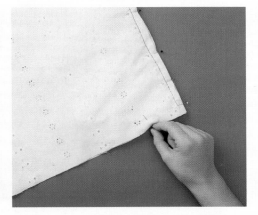

3 Pin runner bottom over top, right sides facing, sandwiching ruffle between layers. Seam panels together, leaving 3-in. (7.5-cm) opening on one long side. Turn right side out; slipstitch opening closed; remove gathering threads; press.

Intermediate Projects

Now that you have mastered some basic beginner techniques, you're ready to move onto something a little more challenging. This section builds upon the skills gained in the beginner section and adds additional techniques to broaden your capabilities.

In this section you can make a beautiful tablecloth with lace panels, ideal for formal occasions; customize mats to add pizzazz to a bathroom; or create a unique window treatment by making triangular valances and curtains.

Intermediate Techniques

Now that you have mastered the basics, you can start to focus on projects that develop your skills further. These projects are slightly more difficult, but the extra challenge will make your project choices even more rewarding.

In this section, you will learn how to make many projects that need fitting and shaping, such as tailored tablecloths, shaped valances, fitted chair cushions, and linings for baskets.

Whichever project you choose, you will learn new skills and create an item to be proud of in your home. For easy reference, the techniques are listed in the order that you find them in the book.

As you sew more, you will probably discover that you become a terrible hoarder of fabrics. Don't panic! Ask fellow sewers if they are able to use a precious piece of fabric that you saved for some, as yet unknown, project. If you really can't avoid taking over a whole room in your house—and have the space—it makes perfect sense to keep your sewing machine and ironing board more or less permanently set up and ready for action. The solution to avoiding chaos is to store all your fabrics neatly so that you can find that special piece again when you really need it.

Make your own duvet cover by stitching two flat sheets together. This is a way to create unique designs, and it is also inexpensive!

HOW TO SHAPE CUSHION PATTERNS

1. Tape newsprint or tracing paper to the top of the seat.
2. Cut the paper into awkward angles to determine the shaping.
3. Lightly trace the shape onto the paper. Neaten the shape.
4. Cut it out. Add seam allowances before cutting the fabric.

USING FUSIBLE HEM TAPE

1. Fusible hem tape is available in several widths and makes a very quick hem.
2. Fold and press a double hem. Cut the tape to the panel width.
3. Position the tape under the top fold of the hem.
4. Press the fabric, fusing the tape according to the manufacturers' instructions.

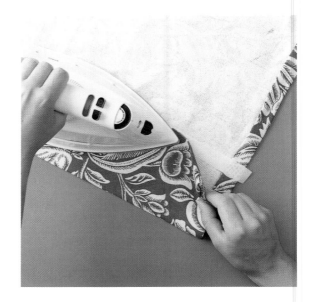

HOW TO SEW A FABRIC CASING

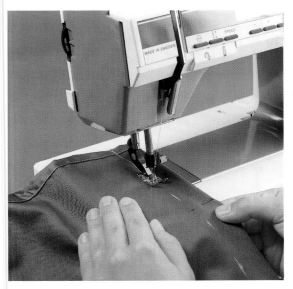

1. To make a casing from shade fabric, add an extra 2 in. (5 cm) per casing when cutting shade.
2. Mark placement of casings. Fold fabric, right sides facing, along each marked line and stitch 1 in. (2.5 cm) from fold to make casing.

HOW TO MAKE PLEATS

1. If you want to match professional-looking box pleats, remember to figure three times the amount of fabric for each pleat.
2. Press each fold and pin each pleat so that you can check the positions of all the pleats together before you start sewing.

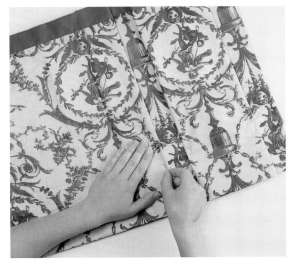

USING GROMMETS ON BLINDS

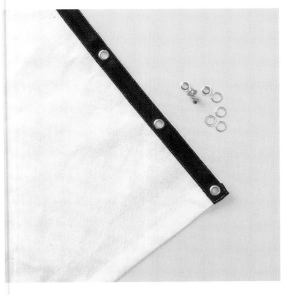

1. Mark position of grommets about every 4 in. (10 cm), working from the edges toward the center.
2. Apply the grommets following the package instructions.
3. Thread twine (or your choice of alternative) through grommets and around the curtain rod.
4. Hang rod and adjust tautness of twine.
4. Secure each end with a double knot on wrong side of grommet.

This soft Roman shade makes a beautifully ethereal treatment for a window. However, with a system of simple cords and rings, it is surprisingly easy to produce the right effect.

Transform plain curtains into elegant features by adding a pleated valance and tiebacks. For a special finishing touch to the room, add a pleated chair pad cover to match.

TECHNIQUES

HOW TO TO PREVENT FRAYING

1. A good technique to prevent seams from fraying is to reinforce stitching by sewing a line of zigzag stitches in the center of seam allowances.
2. Stitch continuously around seamed side and bottom edges.

MAKING A BUTTONHOLE

1. Disappearing markers are used to temporarily mark fabric. (The ink usually disappears within 48–72 hours without washing.) Using a disappearing marker, mark the position of buttonholes.
2. Using either built-in buttonhole-stitch setting or buttonhole attachment of sewing machine, make buttonholes at markings.
3. Insert straight pin at the top of each buttonhole as a stopper before cutting buttonhole. Using a seam ripper, carefully cut through fabric inside sewn buttonholes.
4. Trim off any excess thread.

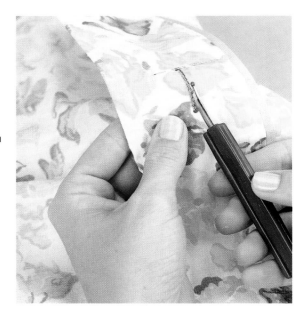

ATTACHING BUTTONS

1. Using a disappearing marker, mark the position where the buttons will be. These should correspond directly with the buttonholes.
2. Using needle and matching thread, hand stitch buttons to fabric in crisscross fashion until secure.

KNOW YOUR NOTIONS!

Notions include buttons, thread, closures, pins, and zippers. Here are some hints and tips about the notions you will find useful for your sewing.

- Self-styling tapes will make curtain headings with gathers or pleats in different styles and depths, including pinch pleats, which give a classic finish. Cut the tape 1 in. (2.5 cm) wider than the curtain, and sew it to the finished panel ½ in. (1 cm) down from the top edge, tucking under ½ in. (1 cm) at each end. Pull up the cords to the desired width and knot them. Do not cut them, as you will need to release the fabric to launder it; just tuck them behind a few of the hooks when hanging the curtain.

- Make a gathering cord that is stronger than ordinary thread. Use crochet cotton, and zigzag it to the fabric just inside the seam line. Make sure you do not catch the cotton with the stitching. Gather up the fabric by gently pushing it along the gathering cord.

- Use metal grommets or clips to create no-sew curtain and drape headings. Grommets come in various sizes, and clips are available in different styles.

- Snap tape is a no-fuss alternative to button or ribbon fastenings—especially on duvet covers.

Make a kraft paper pattern for your chosen valance to suit the width of the rod. Decide on a cut out design and center in the middle of the pattern. Add ½ in. (1 cm) seam allowances. A shaped valance can be made to fit almost every kind of window. Decide which shape best suits the style of the window and the room, then select a fabric that works well with it.

The lining helps the valance hang smoothly, and gives a professional look. Use two coordinating medium-weight fabrics, such as cotton or linen; for best results, use a light-colored solid for the lining.

Fabric-Cutting Guidelines

The valance is hung on a stationary C-rod, which is threaded through openings on the top sides of the valance. Install all of the hardware before measuring for the fabric. Use wide fabric to avoid seaming.

- Measure length between outside edges of installed hardware for valance width. Add to width measurement twice return of rod and 1 in. (2.5 cm) for seam allowances. Cut valance and lining fabrics to determined width by desired height plus 1 in. (2.5 cm) for seam allowances.
- Measure length of contoured edge to determine length of border strip; add 2 in. (5 cm) for mitered corners. Cut border to determined length by border width (about 1 in. (2.5 cm) wide) plus ½ in. (1 cm) on each side for seam allowances.

You'll Need:

✓ Decorator & lining fabrics
✓ Fabric marker or tailor's chalk
✓ Kraft paper & pen
✓ Stationary C-rod
✓ Tape measure, scissors, & straight pins
✓ Needle & thread
✓ Sewing machine
✓ Iron

1 Fold pattern in half and cut it along the center line. Place the half pattern on folded valance fabric; mark and cut out.

2 Measure edge of valance to determine length of border; cut border strip to desired length. If necessary, piece strips to achieve needed length. Try to have seams fall in inconspicuous spots, such as corners.

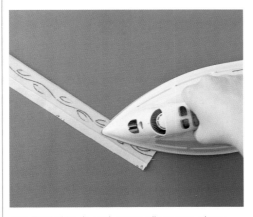

3 Fold ½ in. (1 cm) seam allowance along one long edge of border strip to wrong side of fabric and press.

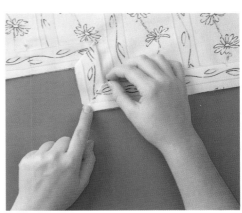

4 Right side facing up, pin border strip along right side of shaped valance edge with raw edges even. Miter corners by folding and pinning excess fabric under diagonally.

5 Stitch along folded edge of border; to secure each corner, shorten stitch length and sew for 1 in. (2.5 cm) on each side of corner; reset to regular stitch length and continue sewing to next corner. If desired, slipstitch diagonal folds in place.

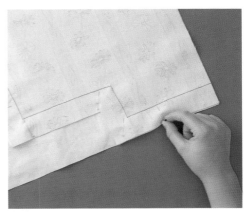

6 Cut lining to valance dimensions. Place valance and lining pieces together, right sides facing, aligning top and side edges of valance with edges of lining. Pin in place.

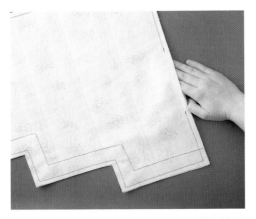

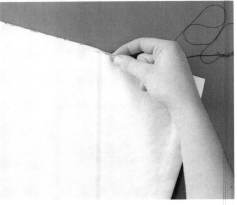

7 Sew valance and lining together with ½-in. (1-cm) seam, following shaped edge. Leave 1½ in. (4 cm)-wide opening at each side of valance top for curtain rod; leave larger, about 3-in. (7.5-cm wide) opening on one side for turning. Trim seam allowances to ¼ in. (5 mm) to reduce bulk.

8 Trim corners diagonally, just outside seamline. Clip into seam allowance at inside corners up to, but not through, seamline. Turn valance right side out. Push corner points out; press flat.

9 Fold under ½-in. (1-cm) seam allowance at top openings; press. Fold under seam allowance at large opening. Slipstitch large opening closed by hand. Thread curtain rod through openings at top of valance and hang.

Crafter's Corner

When sewing the valance and lining panels together, sew around the entire valance without cutting the threads; instead, backstitch at each end of the openings used for the curtain rod and for turning, then continue sewing. After stitching is completed, cut the continuous joining threads, then turn the valance right side out. Use the cut thread ends to slipstitch the turning opening closed.

TRY THIS!

You can customize your valance to make it look stunning. This one pictured has been carefully hand painted, making it a wonderful and inspired alternative to traditional valances.

Sewing an Awning Valance

A valance can be sewn in three pieces and hung on two curtain rods so its bottom extends farther from the window than its top, like an awning.

Install a C-rod with a 3½-in. (9-cm) return at the top of the window frame and a C-rod with a 5½-in. (14-cm) return 10 in. (15 cm) below it. For the fabric width, measure the width of the front of the rod (not the return), and add 1 in. (2.5 cm) for seams. The valance is 13 in. (33 cm) deep, which includes a 2-in. (5-cm) overhang and 1 in. (2.5 cm) for seams. On graph paper, make a pattern for the panels. Draw a 13-in. (33-cm) vertical line. From the bottom of it, draw a 5½-in. (14-cm) horizontal line. From the free end of this new line, draw a 3-in. (7.5-cm) vertical line, parallel to the first. Draw a horizontal line of 3½ in. (9 cm) from the top of the first line, parallel to the second. Draw a line to connect the two free ends. Cut out, check against the hardware, and adjust if necessary.

Mark the "steps" for the bottom of the valance front by dividing the measured width by seven. Starting from the sides, cut four 2½ in. (6 cm)-deep rectangles out of the bottom edge, alternating with full-length steps.

An awning-style–shaped valance projects slightly out from the wall to create a light and airy look. The bold stripes and geometrically shaped lower edge accentuate the depth of this unique window treatment.

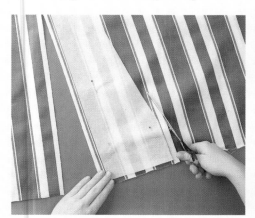

1 Place right sides of fabric together. Cut out two pieces for the side panels, adding ½-in. (1-cm) seam allowance all around. Cut two pieces of lining in the same way. Follow the instructions above and cut out fabric and lining for the front panel.

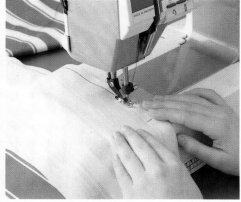

2 With right sides facing, sew diagonal edges of outer side pieces to short edges of outer front piece with ½-in. (1-cm) seams. Sew side and front lining pieces in same manner. Pin outer and lining pieces together, right sides facing.

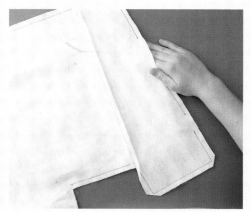

3 Sew side pieces together, leaving openings along outer edges at top and bottom for rods and for turning. Sew main panel pieces together along top and bottom edges. Trim seams, turn right side out, and finish as before.

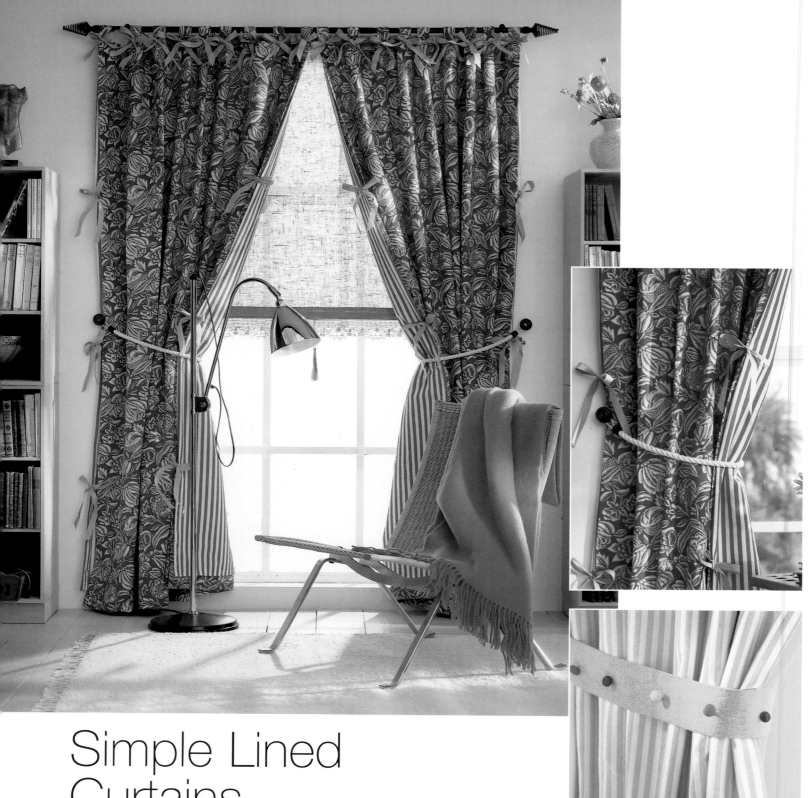

Simple Lined Curtains

Add an extra dash of color and bold decorator style to a window by making curtains lined with a complementary fabric.

Pretty viewed from the outside as well as in, lined curtains are decorative and practical. The added lining weight helps the curtain hang smoothly and also protects the inside curtains from the damaging effects of the sun.

These full-length, tab-top curtains are attached to the lining with ribbons tied to the base of the tabs and with ribbons tied along the sides of the lining and curtain.

By utilizing straight lengths of two different yet complementary fabrics and a wide range of hardware options, you can create an endless number of attractive looks.

Make tiebacks to harmonize with the style of the curtains. The rope tieback enhances the casual elegance of the stripe-lined print curtains. A sunny yellow tieback made from a strip of lining fabric is trimmed with brightly colored buttons. Buttons also attach the lining to the curtain at top and sides.

These tab-top curtains are easy to make from two lengths of coordinating fabric and can be made to fit any window.

Curtain-making Guidelines

The lining's color or pattern should not interfere with the look of the curtain fabric when held up to the light.

- Determine width of curtain and lining panels: Measure length of rod; add 4 in. (10 cm) per panel for 1-in. (2.5-cm) double-fold hem on each panel side; multiply this number by two (for gathers). Divide total by fabric width to get number of fabric widths needed.
- Determine length: Measure from bottom of curtain rod to floor, deduct 1½ in. (4 cm) for tab length. Allow additional 8 in. (20 cm) for 4-in. (10-cm) double hems at bottom. Add 1-in. (2.5-cm) seam allowance along top edge of curtain.
- Determine yardage: Multiply length by number of widths and divide by 36. Add ¼ yd. (23 cm) for safety.
- Measure tab length by pinning fabric strip over rod and marking desired length with pin. Add ½ in. (1 cm) for seam allowance. Cut tabs to measured length by two times desired width plus 1 in. (2.5 cm). To determine number of tabs needed, place tab at top side edges of each curtain and evenly space remaining tabs 6–8 in. (15–20 cm) apart.

You'll Need:

✓ Fabrics for curtain & lining
✓ ¾ in. (2 cm)-wide cotton ribbon
✓ Iron, ironing board, & spray starch
✓ Tape measure & straight pins
✓ Scissors
✓ Sewing machine & thread
✓ Curtain rod
✓ Fusible hem tape

Making Tab-top Lined Curtains

1 Cut curtain, lining, and tabs. Fold each tab in half lengthwise, right sides together. Stitch ½-in. (1-cm) seam, sewing tabs continuously. Cut apart; turn tabs right side out. Press, centering seam in back. Fold and press 1-in. (2.5-cm) double-folded side hems.

2 Press ½-in. (1-cm) double-fold hem along top edge of curtain. Fold tabs in half, ends even. Pin end tabs even with 1-in. (2.5-cm) double-fold side hems. Pin remaining tabs evenly spaced on right side of curtain, aligning ends with top of curtain; edgestitch.

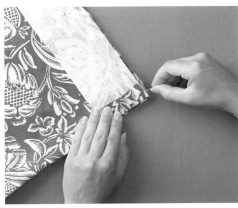

3 Cut 3 in. (7.5 cm)-wide facing strip from curtain fabric, equal in length to width of curtain panel plus 1 in. (2.5 cm) for each side hem. Press under ½ in. (1 cm) along both short ends. Pin facing over tabs along top edge of curtain, right sides together.

4 Stitch through all layers with ½-in. (1-cm) seam. Press facing toward wrong side of curtain, so tabs extend upward. Fold facing under ½ in. (1 cm) along lower edge and pin. Edgestitch along fold and down side hems.

5 Press 1-in. (2.5-cm) double-fold hems along each side of lining and along top edge; edgestitch in place. Cut 20-in. (50-cm) strips of cotton ribbon; fold in half. Sew 1 in. (2.5 cm) at centers to top edge fold.

6 Place curtain on lining, wrong sides together, aligning lining ties with curtain tabs. Wrap ties around base of tabs, making decorative bows. Trim tie ends to give a finished look.

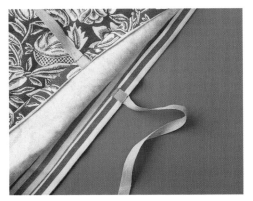

Crafter's Corner

The decorative impact of the finished arrangement relies on the contrast between the curtain and lining fabrics. When arranging the curtains, roll back the sides to expose the lining. If you have a stunning view, buy a curtain rod that is a little wider than the window, so you can draw the curtains wide apart and drape them to the side to frame the vista.

7 Cut six 8-in. (20-cm) lengths of cotton ribbon for each curtain side. Beginning at top corner, pin ribbon pairs in corresponding positions on curtain and lining, evenly spaced at side hems. Sew ties in place. Tie lining to curtain with side ribbons.

8 Insert curtain rod through tabs and hang curtain. Pin double-folded 4-in. (10-cm) hems on curtain and lining; check lengths. Remove curtain; starch and iron folds. Cut fusible hem tape to panel width. Position tape and fuse hems.

Attaching Lining with Buttons

Instead of tying lining to curtain, attach with buttonholes. Make buttonholes 8 in. (20 cm) apart on curtain panel. Sew buttons in corresponding position along inside edges of lining panel. Button curtain and lining together.

TRY THIS!

Refresh the look of old curtains by attaching new fabric curtain panels on top of the existing curtain arrangement with snaps.

Select a fabric of a similar weight and in a color and/or pattern that blends with the existing curtains. Follow the guidelines to make the curtain panels. Attach the panels over your worn or outdated curtains with snaps spaced about 4 in. (10 cm) apart along the top just below the rod and about 1 in. (2.5 cm) in along the sides. The old curtains form a border for the new.

Complete the makeover with new tiebacks and holdback brackets.

You can choose any kind of buttons to attach the lining to your curtains, which such a vast choice you will be able to get the perfect look that you want to make the curtains look great.

Sewing Separate Linings

A simple way to make plain lined curtains is to seam the curtain and lining fabrics together only along the top edge and finish the top with a rod pocket and a ruffled heading.

The beauty of lining curtains in this manner is that when the curtains are hung, the curtain panels can be tied back, leaving the lining panels to hang freely, letting in the light yet providing a degree of privacy.

Follow the cutting guidelines on page 121 to measure and cut the curtain and lining panels. In this curtain arrangement, the right side of the lining fabric faces into the room, just as the curtain fabric does.

Make the lining out of a semi-transparent or sheer lightweight fabric, such as cheesecloth, cotton voile, or lace, to gently filter the sunlight.

These classically styled curtains can be arranged in a number of ways. If you wish to diffuse light or are seeking a degree of privacy, pull back the curtains but leave the sheer lining hanging.

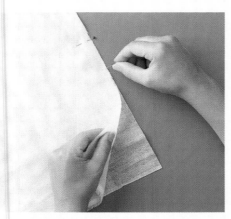

1 Cut out curtain and lining fabrics. Place wrong side of lining fabric on right side of curtain fabric, aligning top edges; pin to within 6 in. (15 cm) of each edge.

2 Double-fold 1-in. (2.5-cm) hems along sides of each panel; pin. Edgestitch hems. Baste curtain and lining together on top edge. Pin ½-in. (1-cm) double-fold hem along top edge; press. Edgestitch hem in place, backstitching at ends.

3 Flip lining over to wrong side of curtain; press seam flat. Mark heading depth and lower rod pocket stitching line with disappearing marker; stitch. Complete lower hem. Insert rod through rod pocket and hang curtain.

Customizing Bathroom Mats

Finding ready-made bath mats in just the color, shape, and size you're looking for is often difficult. But with a minimum of time and expense, you can sew soft and beautiful bath mats perfectly sized and styled for your bathroom.

You can make bath mats in a variety of shapes and styles. Select a solid or printed fabric that picks up the colors of your bathroom, or combine a solid and a print.

Stitching the fabric to a thin sheet of foam rubber provides cushioning and prevents the mat from slipping on smooth tile or linoleum floors. For added texture, machine quilt the fabric and foam layers with a diamond or check pattern.

Follow the same basic steps to sew bath mats in different shapes. Frame a solid-colored rectangular mat with a wide border in a coordinating print. Make this bright flower-shaped mat from yellow and white terry toweling simply by tracing around a small plate for the center and petals. Or try a matching fringe border to give the mat a finished look.

For a durable bath mat, select a densely woven colorfast fabric. Terry toweling, sold by the yard (or meter), is another good choice.

Sewing and Quilting Guidelines
Sewing and home furnishing stores sell foam rubber; a ¼ in. (5 mm) thickness works well for a bath mat.

- If foam rubber "grabs" the sewing machine as you stitch, place a sheet of unprinted newsprint, kraft paper, or shelving paper under foam. If necessary, pin or baste paper to fabric to keep it from shifting. When stitching is completed, tear paper away. If available, sew with quilting foot (also known as walking or even-feed foot).
- Mark quilting lines with tailor's chalk or fabric marker. Use ruler to ensure parallel and even lines. Mark first two quilting rows across center of fabric, then use guide on quilting foot to sew remaining rows. Space lines several inches apart.
- If possible, follow pattern on fabric print for quilting.

You'll Need:

✓ Tape measure, scissors & pins
✓ Sewing machine & thread; iron

For fringed & bordered mat:
✓ Fabrics: print & solid
✓ Sheet of ¼ in. (5 mm)-thick foam rubber
✓ Fringe & thin ribbon or braid for fringed mat

For flower mat
✓ Fabrics: white & yellow terry toweling, yellow and white checkered lining fabric
✓ Fabric marker & string

Making a Bath Mat with a Fringe Border

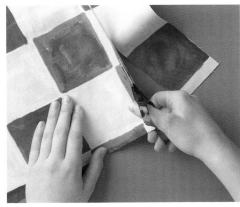

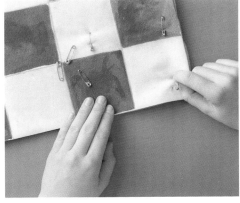

1 Cut fabric to desired dimensions plus ½ in. (1 cm) all around for seam allowances. If using fabric with geometric pattern, follow straight lines of print. Cut foam rubber to same size as fabric less seam allowances.

2 At each edge of fabric, fold under ½ in. (1 cm) to wrong side; press. Place fabric, right side up, on foam rubber; pin to secure. If necessary, use ruler to mark quilting lines on top side of fabric.

3 Stitch along marked quilting lines. Begin by stitching all seams, going in one direction, then remove pins and stitch in opposite direction, across first lines.

4 Pin fringe trim along outer edges of mat, easing fringe around corners for fullness. Stitch along trim heading. Pin and topstitch thin ribbon over seam, mitering at corners.

Making a Bath Mat with a Fabric Border

1 Cut foam and solid fabric. Place foam on wrong side of fabric; edgestitch. Cut four 6 in. (15 cm)-wide border strips to equal mat edges plus 1 in. (2.5 cm). Pin right side of corresponding strip to foam with strip edge 2 in. (5 cm) in from mat edge; stitch ½ in. (1 cm) seam.

2 Fold in seam allowances at ends of strips, then fold border over to front of mat. Fold raw edges of border under scant ½ in. (1 cm); pin in place, covering stitching line. Edgestitch borders in place; handstitch turned-under edges at sides.

Sewing a Flower-shaped Bath Mat

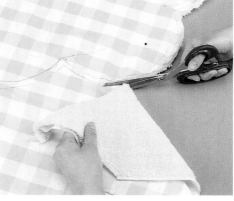

1 On wrong side of checkered fabric, use fabric marker tied to string to mark circle as guides for petals. Lay plate overlapping marked circle and trace around it to mark petal; continue around circle.

2 You may need to adjust arcs to fit full petals around circle. Pin bottom and top fabrics together, right sides facing; stitch along markings, leaving opening for turning. Cut ¼-in. (5-mm) outside seam.

3 Turn right side out; slipstitch opening closed. Trace plate on back side of white toweling; cut out circle. Turn edge under ½ in. (1 cm) and pin circle to center of top. Stitch with tight overedge zigzag stitch.

TRY THIS!

Attractive bath towels of soft, fine-quality terry cloth are perfect for making bath mats. Simply cut foam rubber to size and edgestitch it to the back of the bath towel. Pin a matching fringe with a wide braided heading along the top outside edges of the towel. Then stitch along the top and bottom edges of the heading to secure the fringe to the towel. In no time at all, you'll have a soft, plush bath mat that matches your bath towels perfectly!

Crafter's Corner

Instead of using purchased fringe, you can make your own fringe out of yarn. Begin by cutting the yarn into 5 in. (13 cm)-long pieces. Fold the yarn in half, grouping three or four strands together. Place the folded yarn ½ in. (1 cm) in from the mat edge and machine-stitch it in place just beneath the fold. Continue sewing the folded yarn along the mat edge, stitching continuously and crowding the yarn for desired fullness. To finish, stitch a thin ribbon over the seamline.

Making a Shaped Bath Mat

Make a soft and pretty mat to place in front of the toilet. Cut the mat to fit perfectly around the base of the toilet by tracing the shape onto a thin sheet of paper. Measure the depth and width of the base, then cut slits in the paper and ease it around the curves. Transfer the shape to a sturdier piece of paper and cut it out to make a pattern. Before tracing the shape onto fabric, make sure the fit is right.

Use a soft, plush terry cloth to make an extra-comfortable mat. The mat can be as wide and as long as desired. For best results, extend the mat about 3–4 in. (7.5–10 cm) beyond each side of the toilet base. Cut the fabric and foam rubber to the desired dimensions, then pin the foam rubber to the back side of the fabric. Round the corners of the mat by tracing around a small plate. Bind the two layers together with a contrast binding. Either purchase binding or follow the directions in Step 2 to make your own.

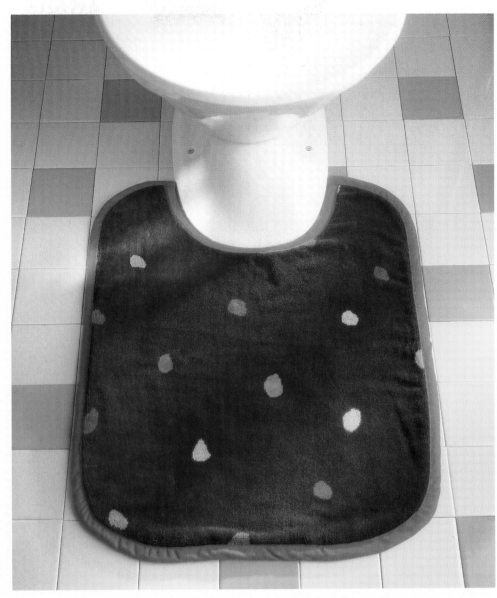

A soft, terry cloth mat custom-made to fit around the front of the toilet provides a warm and comfortable spot to rest your feet. The foam rubber sewn to the underside of the mat helps it stay in place on the floor.

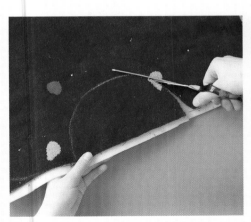

1 Cut fabric and foam. Pin fabric to foam, right side up and edges aligned. With tailor's chalk, trace pattern onto center of one short edge. Trace around small plate to round corners; cut fabric and foam along marks.

2 Measure inside curved edge and outside edge of mat; cut two 2½ in. (6 cm)-wide. bias strips to measured lengths plus 1 in. (2.5 cm). Join strips if necessary for desired length by stitching diagonal short edges together following straight grain.

3 Pin binding to curve on back side; stitch ½-in. (1-cm) seam. Fold binding to front side, turn edge under ½ in. (1 cm), pin, and stitch. Repeat for rest of mat, turning ends of binding under and lapping over ends of binding on curved edge.

Linings for Baskets

A deep basket lined with fabric makes a pretty and practical picnic basket or a special gift presentation. Sewn with inside pockets, these baskets are a pleasing way to showcase food and tableware or a medley of gift items.

The technique for making this simple tie-on, elastic-held liner can be adapted to fit any basket shape. Elasticized pockets sewn to the inside of the liner make it easy to keep the contents in order.

The lined basket is a versatile and useful gift. It can be used as a portable caddy for picnics and shopping or as a decorative accent in the home to store sewing supplies or a craft project in progress. As a bonus, the liner can be easily removed for laundering, which means it has a long life.

To make a drawstring cover for a basket, sew a casing with elastic and ties to secure around basket rim. Sew another casing on opposite edge of cover; thread with ribbon ties and pull to gather cover closed. Coordinate the fabric with its contents, such as a colorful tulip print for a gardener's flower basket.

Purchase a new basket (rectangular is best for a picnic basket) at a craft store or home-and-garden center.

Cutting Guidelines

Measure the basket carefully before cutting the fabric. Before sewing, place the cut fabric pieces in the basket to ensure a proper fit.

- Measure basket's circumference and add 1 in. (2.5 cm). Measure depth and add 5½ in. (14 cm). Transfer dimensions to fabric and cut out two equal pieces for main liner sections.
- Measure length and width of basket bottom; add ½ in. (1 cm) all around. Transfer dimensions to fabric and cut out one piece for liner base. If basket is curved, place paper in basket and trace base; cut out to make pattern. Transfer to fabric; cut out base.
- For pockets, measure width of short side of basket; add 1 in. (2.5 cm) for seams. Determine the pocket depth and add 1 in. (2.5 cm) for seams and 2 in. (5 cm) for casing. Cut two pocket pieces from coordinating fabric.
- To calculate elastic length, encircle elastic around basket opening and mark; subtract 1 in. (2.5 cm) and cut; cut piece in half. For pockets, cut two elastic pieces equal to half pocket width.
- For ties, cut four 14 x 3 in. (35 x 7.5 cm) strips of fabric used for pockets. Fold lengthwise, right sides together, and stitch along raw edges and one short end; turn right side out; press.

You'll Need:

✓ Rectangular basket
✓ 2 coordinating fabrics
✓ ¼ in. (5 mm)-wide elastic
✓ Tape measure
✓ Scissors; seam ripper or tweezers
✓ Thread & straight pins
✓ Sewing machine
✓ iron

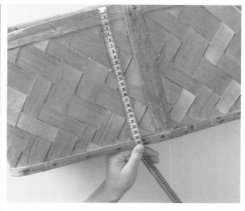

1 Measure circumference and depth of basket with tape measure. Cut out two fabric pieces for lining side and one piece for base as described in guidelines.

2 Place main liner pieces right sides together. At each short edge, measure 5½ in. (14 cm) from top and mark; pin layers together below pin marks. Stitch each side with ½-in. (1-cm) seams from pin marks down. Press seams open.

3 Press under ½ in. (1 cm) along upper edge of liner sections; fold again 1½ in. (4 cm) to wrong side and pin in place.

4 Edgestitch along folded edge of each section. Measure ½ in. (1 cm) up from upper folded edge and stitch second seam on both sections to create casing and ruffle.

5 Cut two pockets; press under ½ in. (1 cm) at each side. Follow Steps 3 and 4 to make casing along top edge of pockets. Center pockets between seams on right side of liner sections, raw edges even at bottom; edgestitch sides up to casing opening.

6 Stitch double row of gathering stitches along lower edge of liner; leave long thread ends. Gently pull on both threads at same time to gather until liner fits base. Pin base to liner, right sides together.

7 Distribute gathers evenly. Sew gathered edge of liner to base with ½-in. (1-cm) seam. After seaming, use seam ripper or tweezers to carefully remove any visible gathering threads on right side.

8 Thread one long elastic piece through casing of each liner section. Pin ends of ties to elastic ends. Sew across openings, catching ends of ties in place.

9 Thread elastic through pocket casings and stitch side edges to secure elastic. Place liner inside basket, aligning fabric ties with each side of handle. Fold top edge of liner over basket opening. Tie ribbon bows around handle. Adjust gathers.

Crafter's Corner

To give the basket a soft, padded bottom, cut out two fabric pieces and one piece of batting for the base. Sandwich the batting between the wrong sides of the fabric pieces and pin the layers together to secure; stitch around base. Treat the padded base as a single piece when sewing it to the main liner sections.

TRY THIS!

Make a southwestern-style jewelry basket fitted with a pretty pouchlike fabric liner.

Measure the top circumference and depth of a round basket. Multiply the depth measurement by 2½ times and double the circumference measurement. Cut out one continuous fabric strip for the liner using measurements. Cut one piece for the base equal to the bottom diameter plus seam allowance. Seam the short ends of the main piece together to make a circle; leave a 1-in. (2.5-cm) opening at center of seam. Fold circular piece in half, wrong sides facing, and sew base to the bottom edge. Thread a decorative cord through the seam opening, insert liner into the basket, and draw the cord to close liner like a bag.

Sewing a Fitted Liner for a Basket

For a lidded basket, a fitted, sewn-on lining is more appropriate than one that is loose and gathered. For proper fit, carefully measure the length, width, and depth of the basket for the liner sides, and the width and length of the bottom for the liner base.

If the fabric you have selected is thin or a little slippery, give it some added body by ironing on a fusible interfacing, following the manufacturer's guidelines.

Measure the dimensions of the basket. Use the measurements to cut a front and back piece, two side pieces, a bottom, and a top piece. Add ½-in. (1-cm) seam allowances all around each piece. Cut corresponding pieces from fusible interfacing, less the seam allowances.

When the fabric pieces are all sewn together, hand sew the liner inside the basket using small stitches and transparent nylon thread. Sew the fabric along the upper edge of the basket liner and then around the outer edge of the fabric lid.

This pretty basket is all dressed up and ready to be taken along on a picnic! Select a stain-resistant fabric for the permanent liner. The liner fabric stays well within the basket edge, making it easy to close the basket lid for carrying.

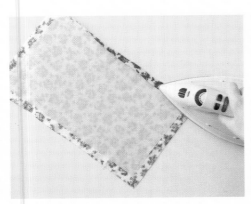

1 Fuse interfacings to wrong side of corresponding fabric pieces. Press edges of lid fabric ½ in. (1 cm) to wrong side.

2 Pin front and back pieces to side pieces, right sides together. Stitch, stopping ½ in. (1 cm) from bottom edges. Press seams open. Sew bottom edge of joined piece to base, right sides together. Press top edges of liner under ½ in. (1 cm).

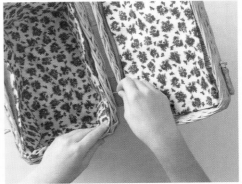

3 Place liner inside basket, aligning corners of liner with corners of basket. Using transparent thread, overcast top edges of liner to inside of basket, through weave. Stitch lid lining to lid around folded edge of fabric.

Roman Shades

A custom-designed Roman shade has a relaxed yet tailored look while providing privacy and controlling the amount of light entering a room.

Despite their stylish and polished look, Roman shades are in fact simple pull-up shades, operated by a system of cords and rings on the back. The shades lay smooth and flat when down; when raised, the shade fabric falls into soft folds. Wooden dowels spaced at equal intervals help the fabric gather and pleat evenly.

The tailored treatment shown gives a window a finished look without overpowering it and is especially appropriate for kitchens, bathrooms, and bedrooms.

This relaxed variation of a Roman shade is easily constructed by omitting the casings and dowels and placing ring tape vertically along the shade fabric. This lets the fabric gather in soft, billowing folds when raised.

The fabric chosen for a tailored Roman shade defines its look. Heavier fabrics will create sharper folds than softer, lightweight fabrics.

Roman Shade Guidelines

Install the curtain rod before measuring for fabric.

- For shade width, measure rod length and add 1 in. (2.5 cm) for each side hem and ½-in. (1-cm) seam allowances for piecing if necessary. For length, measure from top of rod to windowsill; add 2½ in. (6 cm) for rod casing, 4 in. (10 cm) for bottom hem.
- Cut 2 in. (5 cm)-wide strips of interfacing for dowel casings, which are spaced about 8–12 in. (20–30 cm) apart.
- To install shade, insert rod through pocket and mount.
- Anchor one eye screw in window frame to match position of top rings on back of shade and one screw a third down on side of frame. Pull cord end from casing and thread it through screws. Lower shade and adjust cords to equal tension.
- Braid cords and knot at bottom. Use liquid fray preventer or glue on cord ends. Attach awning cleat to center side edge of window frame to wind cord around, holding raised shade in place.

You'll Need:

- ✓ Decorator fabric
- ✓ 2 in. (5 cm)-wide strips of interfacing
- ✓ 10 ½-in. (1-cm) dowels cut 2 in. (5 cm) shorter than shade width
- ✓ 2 ½-in. (1-cm) plastic rings
- ✓ Nylon cording & sewing needle
- ✓ Sewing machine & thread
- ✓ Scissors, measuring tape, & straight pins
- ✓ Awning cleat & 2 eye screws
- ✓ Curtain rod
- ✓ Tailor's chalk

1 Fold up 4-in. (10-cm) hem along bottom edge toward right side of fabric and press. Sew short sides of hem with 1-in. (2.5-cm) seam allowance.

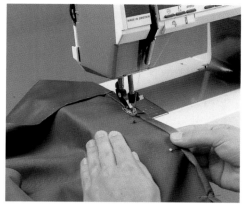

2 Turn hem right side out, encasing side seams; press flat. Fold in ½-in. (1-cm) double hems along both sides and pin. Stitch along folded edge. Press flat.

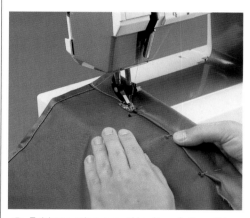

3 Fold top edge over ½ in. (1 cm), then 2 in. (5 cm) and pin in place. Stitch along folded edge to make rod pocket.

4 Mark placement for dowel casings, spacing equally every 8–12 in. (20–30 cm), with first casing covering raw edge of bottom hem. Cut interfacing strips to shade width and pin across shade along markings. Stitch along middle of tapes to attach to shade.

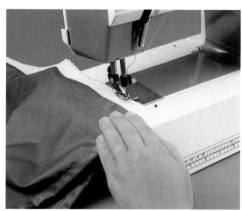

5 To make dowel casings, fold up top and bottom edges of each interfacing strip and sew together with 3-step zigzag stitch.

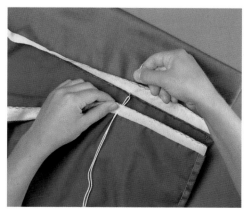

6 Cut length of nylon cord to equal 1½ times shade length plus shade width; thread onto needle. Run cord under casings, about 6 in. (15 cm) from edge, so cord lays flat against fabric. Do not knot cord ends. Repeat on opposite edge of shade.

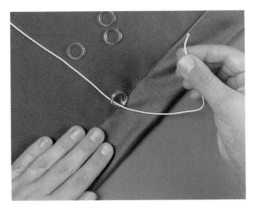

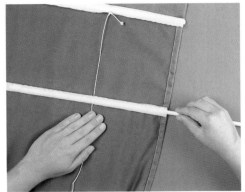

7 Hand baste small plastic rings securely to bottom of top hem in same alignment as cords, approximately 6 in. (15 cm) from edges. Thread cord through rings. Insert one dowel into bottom casing.

8 Bring cord end over casing and knot around stick. Insert remaining dowels; slipstitch casing ends closed. Insert rod into pocket and mount shade. Assemble pull-up system as described on page 45.

Crafter's Corner

To avoid a visible seam on the front of the shade, look for decorator fabrics wide enough to avoid seaming. If your window is very wide, consider making several blinds that can be hung beside one another. For large windows where seaming is required, try to align the shade seams with the vertical mullions (bars) of the window to minimize shadows and hide the seams from the outside. Or try covering the seams with decorative fabric strips or trim.

Sewing Fabric Casings

To form casings from shade fabric, add extra 2 in. (5 cm) per casing when cutting shade. Mark placement of casings. Fold fabric, right sides facing, along each marked line and stitch 1 in. (2.5 cm) from fold to make casing.

TRY THIS!

Add a colorful trim to a solid-colored shade by sewing 4 in. (10 cm)-wide border strips in a contrasting color along the edges of the shade before making the dowel casings. Cut 8½ in. (22 cm)-wide strips, folding a ¼-in. (5-mm) seam allowance on each long edge. Fold the strips in half over the side edges of the shade and pin in place; stitch close to the folded edges of the strips. Repeat on the top and bottom edges. Follow directions to complete shade.

Making a Soft Roman Shade

This easy-to-make variation of the Roman shade has a gathered heading and soft, scalloped folds along the lower edge. The only difference between this soft shade and the basic Roman shade is that the dowel casings are omitted and strips of ring tape are sewn along its length.

To determine the fabric width required, mount the curtain hardware and measure the length of the rod. Multiply this number by 2 and add ½ in. (1 cm) for each side and pieced seam. For fabric length, measure from the top of the rod to the sill, and add 1 in. (2.5 cm) for a narrow bottom hem and 4 in. (10 cm) for the upper rod pocket, heading, and hem. Cut four lengths of ring tape to equal length of shade fabric minus 8 in. (20 cm). Cut pull cords to equal 1½ times the shade length plus the width of the shade.

When installing the shade, gather the fabric evenly along the length of the rod. Follow the guidelines from page 45 to install the pull-up system.

The soft Roman shade gently drapes a window in much the same manner as a curtain. The system of cords and rings lets the shade be raised and lowered at will. Use a lightweight, sheer fabric for an airy look.

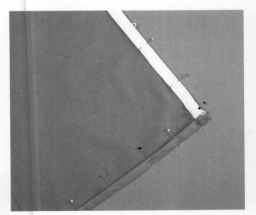

1 Fold in ½ in. (1 cm) along sides of shade and pin ring tape over folds, beginning 1 in. (2.5 cm) from bottom. Vertically pin two more lengths of ring tape evenly spaced across width of shade. Fold bottom edge to wrong side ½ in. (1 cm) twice; pin.

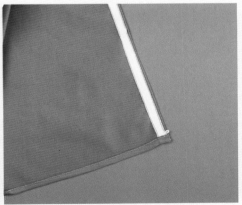

2 Edgestitch along folded edge of bottom hem; press. Stitch along both side edges of tape to secure in place. Repeat to attach all tape strips in place.

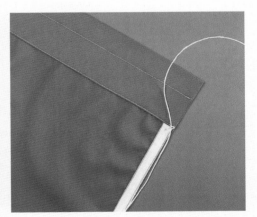

3 Fold top edge 1 in. (2.5 cm) to wrong side; press. Fold over again 3 in. (7.5 cm); edgestitch. Stitch seam 1 in. (2.5 cm) below top edge. Thread cord through bottom ring of each ring tape and knot. Thread cords through rings; assemble system.

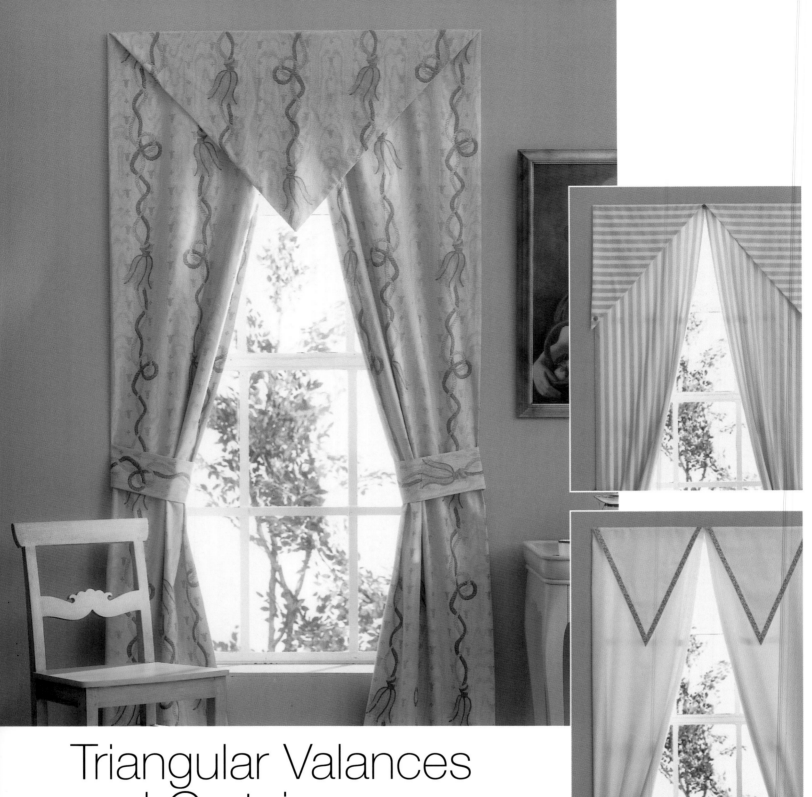

Triangular Valances and Curtains

The strong, angular lines of this simple-to-make window treatment provide a perfect showcase for a striking decorative fabric.

This curtain arrangement is easy to make partly because the curtains are simply flat panels, rather than gathered or pleated, and partly because you need not fuss with multiple curtain rods or stitching rod pockets; instead the triangle valance is sewn directly onto the curtains and then the whole arrangement is hung on a single rod using hook-and-loop fastener tape. The tape is sewn onto the front side of the valance, then folded back to create an instant, no-pocket top edge. Simple fabric tiebacks hold the panels open.

With the basic technique, you can design triangle valances in a variety of different styles. Above, two triangular flaps button onto the curtain panels at the outside edges. Below, trimming the pair of triangle valances with a ribbon border emphasizes their pretty shapes.

Accordion fold each curtain panel, forming three layers per panel to create a self-lining and enough weight for an attractive hang. For each curtain panel, multiply half the window width by three plus 2 in. (5 cm) for side hems. Often the full width of your purchased fabric can accommodate this measurement without joining. If joining is needed, add ½ in. (1 cm) for each seam allowance. For length, measure from the top of the curtain rod to the floor and add 1 in. (2.5 cm) for the top hem and 4 in. (10 cm) for the bottom hems.

Valance Guidelines

Plan the cutting of the valance to center a pretty design element of your fabric.

- Cut valance fabric to window width plus 3 in. (7.5 cm) and to desired length plus 2 in. (5 cm). Fold fabric in half lengthwise, right sides facing. Using straight edge, draw pencil or chalk line connecting top corner of open edge to bottom corner of folded edge; cut along marking. Cut lining fabric in same manner.

- To prevent diagonal cut edges from stretching while sewing, closely pin fabric pieces together. Cut fabric for front of valance following direction of grain and cut lining fabric against grain so pull of lining fabric and front fabric are kept to a minimum.

You'll Need:

✓ Decorator fabric for curtains & valance

✓ Curtain rod

✓ 1 in. (2.5 cm)-wide self-adhesive hook-and-loop fastening tape

✓ Ruler, pencil, or tailor's chalk

✓ Measuring tape, scissors & pins

✓ Sewing machine & matching thread

1 Cut two panels. Sew 2-in. (5-cm) double-folded hem at bottom and 1-in. (2.5-cm) double-folded hem at one side of each panel. If fabric has one-way design, sew hem on outside panel edge. Edge finish opposite cut edge.

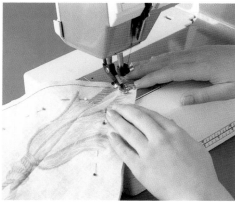

2 Cut two valances. Place pieces together, right sides facing, edges aligned. Sew ½-in. (1-cm) seam along both short sides. Leave top edge unsewn. Trim corner point; turn right side out; press seams flat.

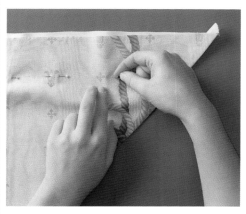

3 Pull top edge of upper valance layer down about ¼ in. (5 mm) and pin in place. Place pins horizontally in fabric, positioned close together about 2 in. (5 cm) below top edge.

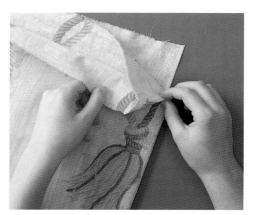

4 Accordion fold each panel lengthwise into thirds so right side faces upward, with hemmed edge and folded edge on top. Each panel should now equal half width of window. Lay curtains side by side, with folded edges toward center.

5 Place valance over curtain panels with top edges aligned. Align center edges of curtain panels with middle of triangle valance. Side valance points will extend out about 1 in. (2.5 cm) on both sides. Pin in place.

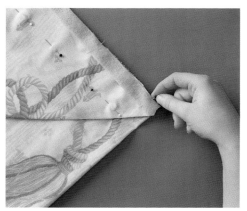

6 Zigzag stitch along upper edge to sew curtains and valance together. Snip off corner points at sides of valance. Pin and sew fastener tape along upper edge. Press tape toward back of curtain and attach to tape on curtain rod. Attach tiebacks.

Trimming a Triangle Valance

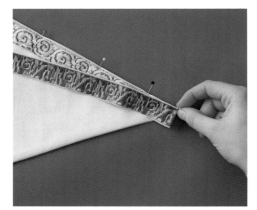 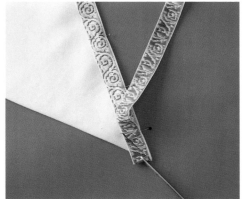 

1 Follow steps to cut and seam valance pieces. Press seams flat. Pin wide ribbon trim along one side edge on front side of valance. At end of triangle point, fold ribbon back. Pin corner fold in place.

2 Stitch across corner of folded ribbon. Begin at pointed end and stitch straight up along center line of triangle to opposite, top edge of ribbon. Cut away excess ribbon on outside of seam. Do not cut valance.

3 Unfold ribbon at corner seam and press flat. Continue to pin ribbon along opposite side edge of valance. Topstitch along inside and outside edges of ribbon. Follow previous instructions to sew valance to curtains.

Crafter's Corner

If the pattern of the fabric on the back side of your valance shows through to the front when light comes in the window, you might prefer to make the back from a solid fabric that blends with your decorator fabric.

To solve the same problem on the curtain panels, sandwich a liner piece between the front and the second layer before sewing the panels and the valance together. If the lining fabric is as heavy as the decorator fabric, cut the decorator fabric to twice, rather than three times, the desired width of each curtain panel and fold the fabric in half with the lining in between.

TRY THIS!

The valance can also be sewn in three triangles. Sew one triangle measuring the window width and two smaller triangles measuring half of the width of the window.

For a striking look, use a striped pattern to contrast with the diagonal lines of the triangle valance. Shown is a striped fabric cut so that the stripes on the corner pieces slant in a different direction from the center piece. The vertical stripes of the curtain panels and tiebacks complete the strong design lines of this window arrangement.

Making Nautical Café Curtains

An interesting alternative to the triangular valance are these café curtains, perfect for a den or study or the cabin of a boat or RV. These ship-shape café curtains are suspended from the rod by rope threaded through a series of grommets attached along the top.

The grommets are small metal hole coverings that are punched into the fabric. These can be found in many sizes and colors at most sewing and craft stores. The tools used to attach the grommets are also available there. Apply the grommets to a fabric edge that has been reinforced with a heavy cotton binding.

The pattern is a basic rectangle that spans the width of the window plus extra for the billowy fullness. To determine the amount of fabric needed, measure the height and width of the window and add an additional 10 in. (25 cm)–20 in. (50 cm) for fullness and 1½in. (3.5 cm) on each side for the hems. Add 1 in. (2.5 cm) on the bottom for a double hem and an extra ½ in. (1 cm) at the top.

A simple short curtain adds a nautical flare to any window when it's attached with sailing twine. Because of the use of hardware and rope, this style of café curtain is a good choice for masculine-styled rooms.

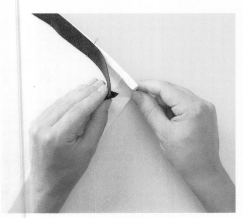

1 Press and stitch ¾ in. (2 cm) wide double hems on sides and ½ in. (1 cm) wide double hems on bottom. Fold and press ½ in. (1 cm) along top edge to right side. Pin ¾ in. (2 cm) binding over folded edge along top; fold binding ends under; stitch.

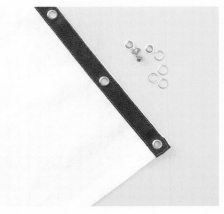

2 Mark position of grommets about every 4 in. (10 cm), working from edges toward center. Apply grommets following package instructions.

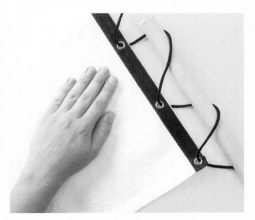

3 Thread twine through grommets and around the curtain rod. Hang rod and adjust tautness of twine. Secure each end with a double knot on wrong side of grommet.

Curtain "Headboards"

Create a fanciful "headboard" by sewing a set of drapes and hanging them over your bed to lend personality and add a customized look to your bedroom.

This elegant headboard is created by hanging curtains from standard curtain rods attached to the wall. Style your headboard in just the same way as you style traditional full-length curtains. Unlined, gathered curtains are the simplest to make; adding a shirred back panel and valance makes the headboard look even more realistic. A fabric-sash topping echoes the bow tiebacks.

The headboard's pronounced height and abundance of fabric generously contributes color and texture to your bedroom decor.

Plain curtains caught with cord tiebacks and decorated with tasseled cord sashing create a handsome combination for a casual ambience. Omitting the valance and background panel leaves a streamlined design requiring less fabric and sewing time.

The simplest way to create layered treatments is to use a triple curtain rod. If a triple rod is unavailable, combine a single with a double curtain rod.

Cutting Guidelines

To determine the width of the back panel, side curtains, and valance, measure the length of the respective rod; for fullness, multiply this measurement 2½ times for heavyweight fabrics, and 3 times for sheer or lightweight fabrics. Add side hems: 3 in. (7.5 cm) for back panel, and 6 in. (15 cm) for curtains and valance. Add ½ in. (1 cm) for all joining seams. Divide total number by fabric width for number of fabric lengths needed.

- To determine rod pocket allowance: Double height of rod and add ½ in. (1 cm) for easing.
- To determine cutting length of back panel and curtain: Measure distance from top of rod to floor. Add rod pocket allowance, plus ½ in. (1 cm) for turning and 2 in. (5 cm) for hems.
- To determine valance cutting length: Add desired length to doubled heading allowance, plus rod pocket allowance, plus 2-in. (5-cm) hem.
- For yardage: Multiply cutting lengths by number of lengths needed, including extra for tiebacks and valance sashes and loops. Divide total by 36.
- If curtain is used without valance, add heading to rod casing: Double desired height of heading and add rod pocket allowance, plus ½ in. (1 cm) for turning.

You'll Need:

- ✓ Triple curtain rod or single & double rod
- ✓ Curtain fabric
- ✓ Tape measure, scissors, pins & hand-sewing needle
- ✓ Sewing machine & matching thread
- ✓ Stepladder

Sewing Valances

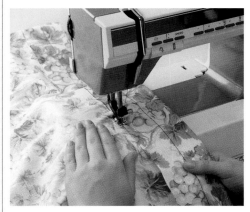

1 Fold and stitch bottom and side hems of each valance. Press ½ in. (1 cm) to wrong side along upper edge. From folded edge, mark depth of rod pocket plus heading allowance. Press fabric to wrong side at marking. Stitch marked and folded edges.

3 Fold loop ends under. Pin three loops (one loop at each edge and one centered) to front of each valance, along rod pockets. Sew across loop ends so stitches align with stitching of rod casing.

Sewing Back & Side Panels

Sew ¾-in. (2-cm) double hems on side edges of back and side panels. Press lower hems up ½ in. (1 cm), then 1½ in. (4 cm); stitch. Press under ½ in. (1 cm) along upper edges; fold to depth of rod casing; press, and stitch along folded edge.

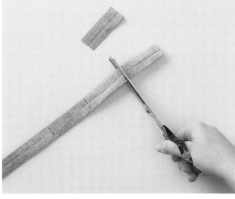

2 Cut four 6 x 55 in. (15 x 140 cm) fabric strips for sashes and tiebacks. Fold lengthwise, right sides facing; sew; turn right side out. Cut 16½ x 2 in. (42 x 5 cm) strip for loops. Sew lengthwise, right sides facing; turn right side out and press. Cut six strips 2¾ in. (7 cm) long.

4 On each valance panel, lace one sash through loop at outside edge; pin and hand sew sash end in place. Lace sash through remaining two loops toward center. Use two remaining strips for tiebacks.

Hanging "Headboard"

1 Working on stepladder, remove inside rod and thread through rod casing of back panel; reinstall rod. Adjust panel gathers evenly across width of rod.

2 Remove middle rod and slide through both side curtain casings. Reinstall rod and adjust gathers. Pull curtains to sides and catch with tiebacks. Fasten tiebacks either to bedposts or to tieback hooks attached to wall.

3 Remove outer rod and thread through both valance casings. Reinstall rod. Adjust gathers and heading so folds fall evenly across width of arrangement. At center, tie sash ends into a bow that sits at middle of valance.

TRY THIS!

The basic faux-window treatment can be altered to create an infinite variety of styles. An asymmetrical arrangement is ideal where a two-paneled curtain would be too overwhelming, such as for a corner placement. Join lengths and make a single curtain panel with a gathered heading.

Cut two 6 in. (15 cm)-wide strips of contrasting fabric using the width of the curtain panel plus 1 in. (2.5 cm). Fold the strips in half and sew to make the sash and tieback. Cut an 8¼ in. (21 cm)-long strip of panel fabric and cut it into three 2¾ in. (7 cm)-long pieces; fold and seam to make loops and attach them along the seams of the rod pocket 1 in. (2.5 cm) from the side edges and at the center. Thread the sash across the curtain and stitch the ends at both sides to secure. Draw the curtain over to one side and gather in the tieback. Attach the tieback to the wall using a tieback hook or hook-and-loop fastener tape.

Crafter's Corner

A change of trim or detailing can create an entirely new look for your dull and dreary headboard. Make the tiebacks and sashes stand out from the curtain by using contrasting fabric, or wide, glossy ribbon, or decorative cord.

Pretty trimmings, such as border braids, fringes, and tassels, can all accentuate the curtain arrangement with color, texture, and also movement. For a visual counterpoint, place an interesting bow or tassel at the curtain's center.

Creating a Curtain Canopy

This unusual canopy treatment is made from a single length of fabric, folded and seamed together. A casing is sewn across the middle, and the canopy is hung on a rod projecting from the wall.

Complete bed-canopy kits are available from home stores. Also, metal or wooden poles can be cut to length and inserted into fixtures such as barrel brackets that are screwed to the wall and project out a number of inches; discuss the alternatives with a salesperson at a good hardware store. For a tapered effect, cut the top pole 20 in. (50 cm) and the two holdback poles 15 in. (38 cm).

To determine the amount of 45 in. (1.15 m)-wide fabric needed, measure from the top pole, down over the holdback pole, to the desired length, then multiply by four. Select from the many pole ends and finials available, or design your own by gluing on decorations you have found or purchased.

A cozy canopy bed adds visual interest and scale to a bedroom. The still life framed within the curtains grounds the arrangement visually, and the golden star finials accentuate the graceful drape of the fabric.

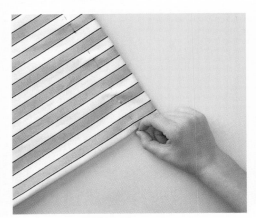

1 Install all hardware. Fold fabric in half crosswise, right sides together. Stitch along cut edges, leaving opening for turning; trim corner seam allowances. Turn right side out. Press and slipstitch opening closed.

2 Fold stitched canopy piece in half crosswise. From folded edge, measure down rod pocket allowance and pin mark. Stitch along marking to form rod casing.

3 Slide casing over rod. Attach brass star finial at end. Attach remaining finials to holdbacks; if necessary, add glue to secure. Drape sides of canopy over holdbacks and secure with double-sided adhesive tape.

Tailored
Table Covers

Turn a plain, round table into a beautiful room accent with a gathered two-piece table covering.

A pretty table skirt adds color and pattern to a decorating scheme. The soft gathered look is easy to achieve using sew-on shirring tape with built-in loop fasteners.

For a perfect fit, the skirt attaches to the made-to-measure top piece with hook-and-loop fastener tape and can be easily detached for laundering or a change of decor.

Make the skirt and the top from the same fabric to create the appearance of a single treatment, or sew them from coordinating fabrics, such as the striking blue-and-white stripe and delicate floral shown, for a tailored layered effect.

Above: Use the same fabric for the top and the skirt to make a beautiful table covering that takes center stage.

Consider making several coordinating skirts and top pieces to mix and match. For best laundering, don't cut the excess cords on the shirring tape so you can release the gathers from the skirt fabric.

Fabric-Cutting Guidelines

Use standard two-cord shirring tape and stitch a strip of loop tape over it after it is gathered.

- To estimate skirt fullness, multiply circumference of round table (or sum of four sides for square or rectangular table) by two, then add 1 in. (2.5 cm) for seams. For length of skirt, measure from tabletop to ½ in. (1 cm) above floor, then add 1½ in. (4 cm).
- Join fabric panels to achieve desired width, unless you can cut skirt along length of fabric.
- Cut hook tape to circumference of table. Cut shirring tape to twice circumference.
- For circular top, measure diameter and add 1 in. (2.5 cm) for seam, then cut fabric square to this measurement. Fold square in quarters. Tie tailor's chalk to string, hold string at double-folded corner, and draw arc connecting two outer corners; cut.
- For rectangular table skirt, cut top to length and width of tabletop plus ¾ in. (2 cm) on each side. Cut four sides with widths equal to each side of table plus 1 in. (2.5 cm) and length equal to table height plus 1½ in. (4 cm). Cut four square gusset pieces equal to table height plus 1½ in. (4 cm).

You'll Need:

- ✓ 2 decorator fabrics
- ✓ Hook-and-loop shirring tape
- ✓ ¾ in. (2 cm)-wide hook-and-loop fastener tape
- ✓ Tape measure, straight pins, scissors, tailor's chalk, & string
- ✓ Sewing machine & thread; iron

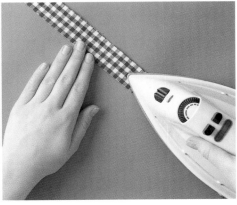

1 Cut circular top piece. Machine-baste around circumference ½ in. (1 cm) in from edge. Cut 2½ in. (6 cm)-wide fabric band to equal table's circumference plus 1 in. (2.5 cm); stitch ends to form ring. Fold band in half lengthwise, wrong sides together, and press.

2 Pin band to right side of top piece with raw edges even. Using basting stitches as guide, sew band to top piece with ½-in. (1-cm) seam. Fold band out and press seam open.

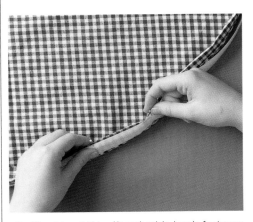

3 Pin strip of ¾ in. (2 cm)-wide hook-fastener tape to band on right side, covering entire width of band. Stitch along top and bottom edges of tape to secure in place. Cut fabric for skirt. Press and sew ½-in. (1-cm) double-folded hem along bottom of skirt.

4 Press ½ in. (1 cm) along top edge of skirt to wrong side. Pin wrong side of shirring tape over top edge ¼ in. (5 mm) below fold; stitch along top and bottom edges of tape, being careful not to catch cords. Apply loop-fastener tape over gathered skirt to attach to hook tape on table top.

5 Sew side edges of skirt together, right sides facing, with ½-in. (1-cm) seam, keeping shirring cords away from seam. Pull shirring tape cords to gather fabric to fit top piece. Knot cord ends to secure.

6 Adjust gathering to distribute fullness evenly. Attach gathered skirt to top piece with loop tape. Adjust position of gathered skirt to ensure that hook-and-loop tape is not visible.

Making a Rectangular Table Cover with Tailored Skirt and Gussets

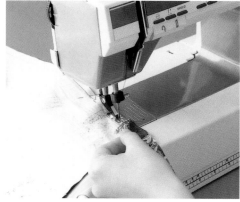

1 Cut top piece, gussets, and sides. Sew one side piece to gusset along one seam, stopping ½ in. (1 cm) from top; press seam toward side. Sew adjacent side piece to gusset, stopping at previous seam.

2 Attach all sides and gussets. Draw arc connecting lower corners of sides across gusset; cut along marked arc. Sew double-folded ½-in. (1-cm) hem.

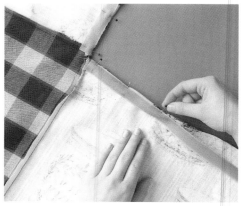

3 On top edges of side pieces, fold ½-in. (1-cm) seam allowance to wrong side. Pin and stitch loop-fastener tape along folded edges. On right side of top piece, pin and stitch hook-fastener tape along edges. Press tapes together to attach skirt.

TRY THIS!

With a made-to-fit top piece and side pieces attached with hook-and-loop fastener tape, you can create table coverings in many different styles. In this stunning treatment, the top piece and front under panel are cut from one fabric, and the sides, back, and decoratively shaped front flap are made from a coordinating fabric. The shaped front is cut and sewn from two layers of fabric, then turned right side out and pressed for sharp, finished cut edges.

The geometric cutout of the front over-piece is suggested by the fabric's pattern; other patterns, such as florals, would look better cut with curving or scalloped shapes.

Crafter's Corner

Finding a table pad just the right size to place beneath a fitted table skirt can be difficult. For an easy solution, make a combination table skirt and pad by either cutting and sewing an old wool blanket or fusing a sheet of fleece to the underside of the top piece for a layer of padding and protection.

Adding Decorative Details

The straight lines and sides of square and rectangular table skirts invite decorative extras. This handsome fitted cloth has contrast piping, inverted corner pleats, and faced triangles.

Buy piping or make your own by covering cable cord with bias-cut fabric strips. The strip's width is the cord's circumference plus 1½ in. (4 cm). Cut cord and bias strip to a length equal to the table's perimeter plus a couple of inches (about 5 cm) for a safety margin. To make piping, fold bias strip in half lengthwise, wrong sides facing; place cord within fold and machine baste with zipper foot close to cord.

Determine size and number of triangles for your table. Cut two pieces for each triangle; stitch together, leaving top edge open.

After stitching top of skirt, sew ¾ in. (2 cm)-wide loop-fastener tape over seam on right side. Stitch hook fastener tape along the outside edge of the piping on the right side of the top piece, then press the tapes together to form complete table covering.

Piping sewn to the edge of the top piece of this table treatment delineates its shape, the inverted corner pleats give the skirt a soft, slanting drape that echoes the lines of the triangle edging.

1 Cut top to length and width of tabletop plus ¾ in. (2 cm) on each side. Pin piping to right side of top with raw edges even; clip piping seam allowance at corners. With zipper foot, machine stitch piping close to cord.

2 Cut fabric for skirt to perimeter of table plus 48 in. (1.22 m) by table height plus 1¾ in. (4.5 cm). Double-fold ½-in. (1-cm) hem along lower edge; edgestitch. Cut triangle pieces; stitch two pieces together, right sides facing. Turn right side out; press.

3 Form pairs of 3 in. (7.5 cm)-deep inverted pleats at skirt corners. Pin triangles along upper edge between corners; stitch to hold pleats and triangles. Sew loop tape along top edge of skirt, hook tape on outside edge of piping.

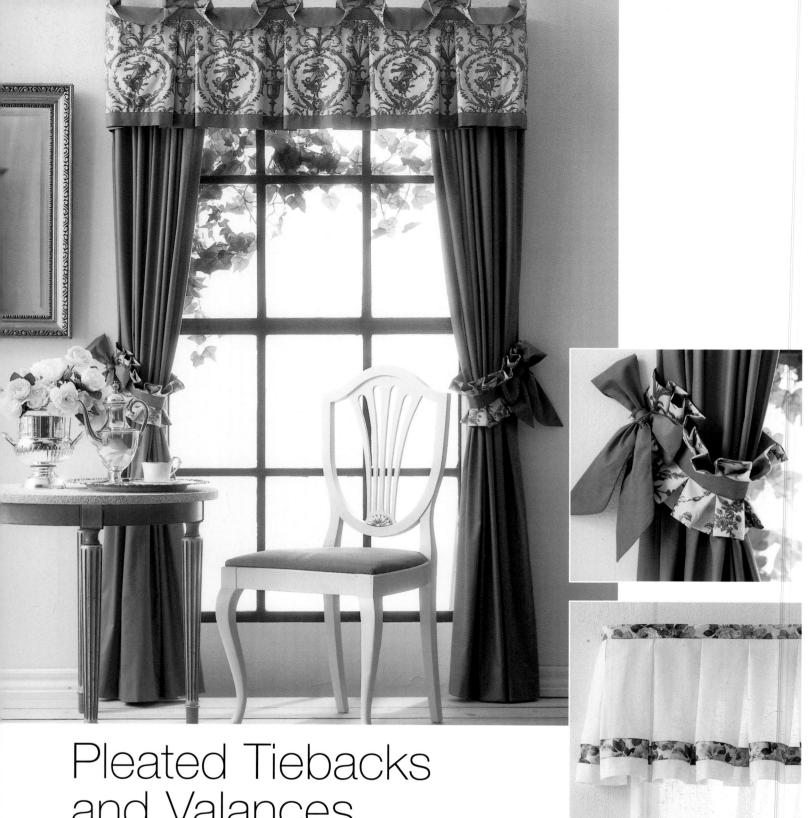

Pleated Tiebacks and Valances

Transform simple curtain panels into an elegant window treatment by adding a contrasting pleated valance and tiebacks. The results are very easy to duplicate.

To create this gracious, welcoming window treatment, combine solid-colored drapery fabric with an elegant contrasting print. The featured fabric has a design that has been enhanced by the pleating process in the valance, header, and tiebacks. Use a fabric that holds a pleat crisply, such as cotton chintz. A fabric that is too thin or too thick won't maintain the pressed pleats.

Achieving this decorator look has more to do with careful measuring, pinning, and folding than with complicated sewing techniques.

Different looks can be created using pleats in different ways. Pleated and bow-trimmed tiebacks add a polished finish to curtain panels. An unbleached linen valance trimmed with chintz floral bands has a casualness that would fit in any room of a country-style home.

Welting can be inserted in the seams of any size or shape of pillow. Almost any fabric can be used to make the welting, but it should be the same weight and have the same care requirements as the pillow cover. Prewash fabric to avoid shrinkage or discoloration in subsequent laundering. If combining light and dark fabrics, pretest them for colorfastness.

Cotton or polyester cord comes in diameters ranging from ⅛ in. (3 mm) to 2 in. (5 cm) and can be purchased at fabric stores. Buy enough cording to go around the perimeter of the pillow plus extra for finishing the ends.

Cutting Guidelines

Fabric for welting is cut on the bias so it can conform to curved edges. Make your own bias strips or purchase ready-made bias binding.

- Cut pillow-cover pieces ½ in. (1 cm) larger all around than finished pillow.
- To determine cut width of bias strips, measure circumference of cord and add 1 in. (2.5 cm).
- Join bias strips to make continuous length equal to perimeter of pillow plus 3 in. (7.5 cm): Pin two strips right sides together, with straight grain ends placed edge to edge. Stitch with ¼ in. (5 mm) seam; press open.
- Cut cord to same length as finished continuous bias strip.
- If using purchased bias tape, open tape and press it flat before encasing cord.

You'll Need:

✓ Fabric for pillow cover & welting
✓ Pillow form
✓ Cording
✓ Tape measure
✓ Scissors
✓ Straight pins
✓ Sewing machine & thread

1 Cut two 17-in. (43-cm) square pieces of fabric for 16-in. (40-cm) square pillow, including ½-in. (1-cm) seam all around. Round corners either freehand or using plate as guide; mark with pencil. Cut corners along markings.

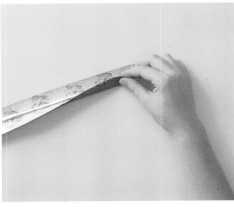

2 Join bias strips cut from welting fabric to make a length of 67 in. (1.7 m). Cut cording to same length. Press strip flat; place cord along center on wrong side of fabric. Fold fabric around cord with raw edges even. Pin if desired.

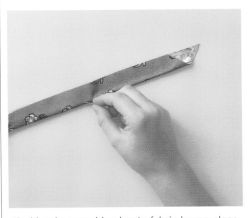

3 Hand or machine baste fabric layers close to cording; do not let cording twist inside. If machine basting, use zipper foot to get stitching line close to cord without stitching into it.

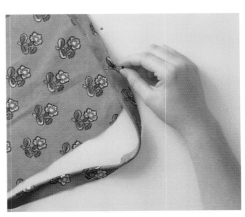

4 Pin basted welting to right side of one pillow-cover piece, matching all raw edges. Place pins closer together in corners, easing welting around curves. Welting should be smooth but not taut.

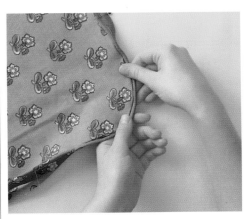

5 At curved corners, clip welting seam allowance at intervals as needed to make welting lay flat. Check that welting lays properly around corners by folding welting under at corners from right side of fabric.

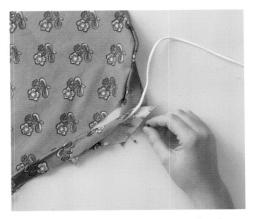

6 Where ends meet, remove some basting stitches and pin the ends of bias strip together, right sides together, so strip fits within pillow dimension; stitch ends following straight grain. Trim seam allowance; press seam open.

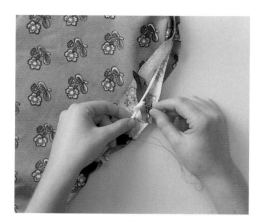

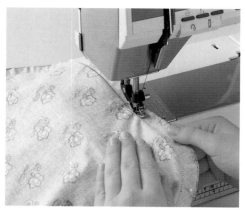

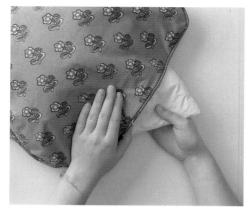

7 Tie cord ends together in small square knot so cording fits within pillow dimension. Cut cord ends. Continue basting welting to pillow front.

8 Right sides facing, pin both pillow pieces together; sew, stitching inside previous cord-stitching line (closer to cord). Leave opening along one edge. If desired, trim seams.

9 Turn cover right side out. Insert pillow form into cover. Adjust and smooth cover over pillow form. Slipstitch opening closed.

Crafter's Corner

To make it easier to open and close a pillow cover for laundering, sew strips of hook-and-loop fastener tape, snaps, or a zipper in the seam instead of stitching the opening closed. The pillow cover can also be sewn with an opening on the back side for easy removal. To do this, make the back from two pieces and overlap the edges at the center.

TRY THIS!

Vary the look of the welting with soft shirring: Cut the cording 10 in. (25 cm) longer than the pillow perimeter to be welted; cut the bias strip to twice the pillow perimeter. (If desired, you can cut fabric strips with the grain rather than on the bias.) Wrong sides together, fold the strip in half lengthwise and lay the cord along the fold. Using a zipper foot, stitch over the cording about 3 in. (7.5 cm) from the end, then stitch close to the cord for about 10 in. (25 cm); stop the machine with the needle in the fabric. To shirr, gently pull the cord toward you while pushing the fabric behind the presser foot back to the sewn end. Stitch and shirr 10 in. (25 cm) at a time until the gathered length equals the pillow perimeter. Pin the shirred welting in place, matching raw edges, then trim the cord and sew the ends together.

Edging with Twisted Cord

Trim pillows with a thick twisted cable cord for a smart decorator finish. This type of cording, which is attached to a fabric tape for stitching, is sold in fabric and sewing stores. Stitch the tape into the seam allowance between the pillow front and back pieces, leaving the cording on the right side just outside the seamline. Stitch the trim in place as close to the cording as possible so the fabric tape is concealed within the cover and only the decorative cording is visible.

Begin by machine stitching the cord to the right side of one pillow-cover piece. Then stitch the two layers of the cover together, sewing as close to the cord as possible. If the fabric tape is showing in any spots after seaming, baste the fabric cover over it.

Update your decor with new pillows. For an easy and attractive alternative to piping, purchase decorative twisted cording with a fabric tape designed to be stitched into the pillow seam.

1 Pin cording tape to right side of one pillow-cover piece, raw edges even with tape edges. Pin cording around entire perimeter of pillow, being sure not to pull cover fabric at corners.

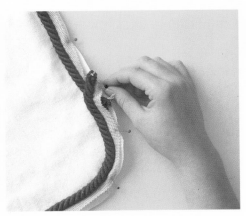

2 Using zipper foot or sewing by hand, stitch cording as close to cord as possible. Overlap ends and stitch together. Trim off excess cord.

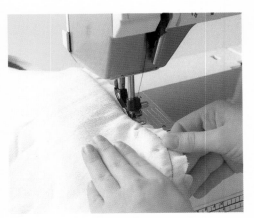

3 Stitch top and bottom of pillow cover together, right sides facing and raw edges aligned, leaving opening along one edge. If desired, trim seams. Turn cover right side out, insert pillow form, and slipstitch opening closed.

Simple Duvet Covers

This quick sewing method of stitching two flat sheets together to make a duvet cover for a favorite comforter is an easy and economical way to give your bedding a fresh new look.

A duvet cover is both decorative and protective and has a stylish closure along one edge that lets the cover be easily removed for laundering or redecorating.

A pair of sheets with generous widths is ideal to use for the cover— no piecing is required. Simply stitch up the sides and bottom, then add buttonholes and buttons along the broad, decorative top hem to create the closure edge. Look for two colored sheets that blend best with your bedroom decor.

Duvet covers offer many closure options. The cover made from plain blue sheeting is held closed with mother-of-pearl snaps attached along the open edge. The striped cover closes with 12-in. (30-cm) lengths of grosgrain ribbon sewn along the top edges and tied into bows.

Select lightweight cotton or cotton-blend sheets. Avoid sheets marked "irregular," because the sheet may be cut off-grain.

To determine the cutting size of the cover, measure the duvet to be covered and add 2 in. (5 cm) to the width and 1 in. (2.5 cm) to the length. Purchase two flat sheets in the next larger size to the cutting dimension. For example, for a 76 x 86 in. (1.93 x 2.18 m) duvet, purchase two full-size (80 x 105 in./2 x 2.26 m) flat sheets; for a 86 x 86 in. (2.18 x 2.18 m) duvet, purchase two queen-size (90 x 110 in./2.28 x 2.54 m) flat sheets; for a 101 x 86 in. (2.56 x 2.18 m) duvet, purchase two king-size (110 x 110 in./2.54 x 2.54 m) flat sheets.

Sewing Guidelines

While buttons, ribbons, and tabs make stylish closures, hook-and-loop tape fasteners and zippers offer quick-change convenience as well.

- Before cutting, wash and dry all-cotton and flannel sheets to preshrink. Press out wrinkles.
- When cutting fabric, cut bottom and side edges, leaving broad hemmed top border in place for closure edge. Lay sheet on large, flat work surface. Use scissors or rotary cutter and ruler to cut fabric. Cut straight across bottom of sheet to remove double bottom hem.

You'll Need:

- ✓ 2 coordinating flat sheets
- ✓ Rotary cutter, ruler & cutting mat
- ✓ Sewing machine & matching threads
- ✓ Hand-sewing needle & straight pins
- ✓ Disappearing marker
- ✓ Flat buttons
- ✓ Scissors & seam ripper

1 Measure and mark cutting dimensions, include 1-in. (2.5-cm) seam allowances along sides and bottom edge of sheets. Lay ruler along markings and roll rotary cutter next to ruler edge to cut fabric.

2 With right sides together and all edges aligned, pin sheets together along bottom and sides. Machine-stitch along bottom and side edges with 1-in. (2.5-cm) seam. Shorten stitch length as you pivot and turn at corners.

3 To prevent seams from fraying, reinforce stitching by sewing line of zigzag stitches in center of seam allowances. Stitch continuously around seamed side and bottom edges.

4 To reduce bulk, use scissors to clip seamed corners. Cut through corners at 45° angle, ⅛ in. (3 mm) away from straight stitching. Turn duvet cover right side out.

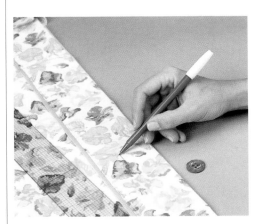

5 On front of cover, using disappearing marker, mark position of buttonholes approximately 6 in. (15 cm) apart along center of top decorated edge. Make lines ⅛ in. (3 mm) longer than diameter of buttons.

6 Using either built-in buttonhole-stitch setting or buttonhole attachment of sewing machine, make buttonholes at markings. Refer to sewing-machine manual for specific guidelines.

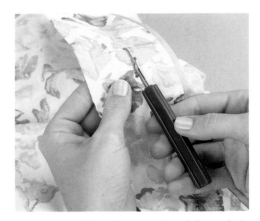

Crafter's Corner

To offset the cost of purchasing two designer top sheets, consider using a plain sheet for the back of the duvet cover. Another alternative is to use a plain sheet for the top and add a decorative border, like a ribbon or lace trim, along the top edge, or stitch a coordinating piping, welting, or ruffle in the seams.

7 Insert straight pin at top of each buttonhole as a stopper when cutting buttonhole. Using seam ripper, carefully cut through sheet inside sewn buttonholes. Trim off any excess thread.

8 Lightly mark for buttons in corresponding positions along inside top edge of back cover. Using needle and matching thread, hand stitch buttons to fabric in crisscross fashion until secure.

TRY THIS!

Buttons add a flourish to store-bought pillowcases. Sew three evenly spaced buttons about 1 in. (2.5 cm) from the seamed end of the pillowcase. Then machine stitch three evenly spaced buttonholes in the same alignment on the front side of the open edge. Hand stitch buttons in the corresponding positions along the inside hem of the open edge. Insert pillow and button.

For a fashionable bed ensemble of duvet cover and pillows, select pillowcases that match or complement the sheets used for the duvet cover.

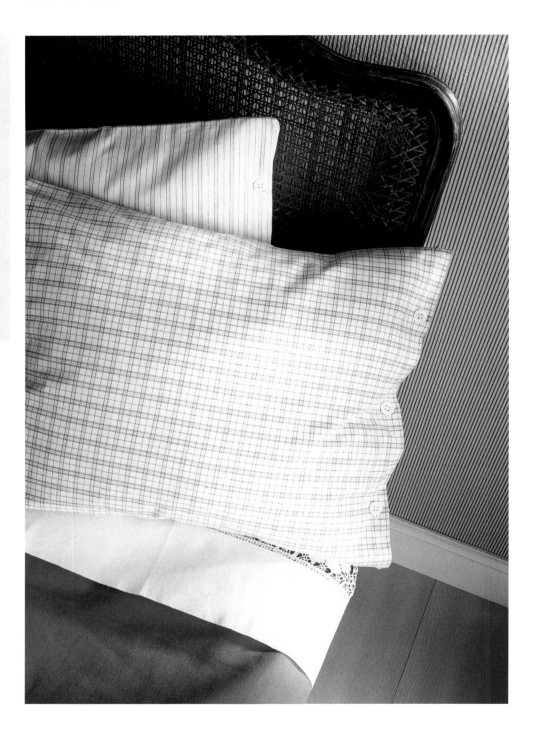

Sewing a Flanged Sham

Gather an assortment of pillows to arrange on your bed and coordinate with your duvet cover. The chic pillow sham featured here has a decorative flange border and a discreet lapped back opening.

To make a sham for a standard size bed pillow, cut two fabric pieces measuring 25 x 31 in. (63.5 x 78 cm) for the front and back; cut one smaller piece measuring 10½ x 25 in. (26 x 63.5 cm) for the flap extension. The cutting dimensions include ½-in. (1-cm) seam allowances.

Make a double 1-in. (2.5-cm) hem on one of the short sides of the back piece to create the pillow opening. When the front and back pieces are pinned together for seaming, the side front edge will extend 2 in. (5 cm) farther than the hemmed back edge. Make a narrow hem on one long side of the extension, then stitch the raw edge to the extended front side. When the sham is turned right side out, the extension piece should lay inside the sham.

A flanged pillow sham with a narrow ribbon trim will add a stylish, contemporary finish to your bed. Use a complementary solid-color fabric for the sham and coordinate the trim with other design details in your bedroom decor.

1 On short edge of back piece, press under 1-in. (2.5-cm) double hem; edgestitch. Pin front to back, right sides together and raw edges even. Pin hemmed extension to extended front edge, right sides together. Seam around sham.

2 Turn sham right side out; press seams flat. To form flange, stitch around sham 2 in. (5 cm) from outer edge, using seam gauge on machine as guide; push folded back edge to side while working, to avoid sewing over opening edge.

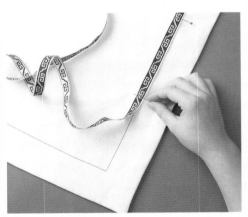

3 Pin ribbon trim along flange seamline, mitering corners; topstitch along both edges of ribbon, stitching in same direction to prevent wrinkles; fold down back edge of opening to avoid stitching opening closed.

More Experienced Projects

This section is for the more accomplished sewer. Now that you have mastered the basics, try some of these projects that could completely transform your home.

You can make fabric shutters to create a fantastic look or simply to have some privacy. Make cushions with tufts and tassels for the chairs inside your home or for those on the patio. Or give your bedroom a fresh new look by making a reversible bedspread.

More Experienced Techniques

One of the focuses of this section is learning how to add layers of detail to your projects. You will find out how to use buttons, welting, and zippers effectively to make sophisticated pillows, box cushions, and bolsters. You will see examples of how to combine fabric colors and patterns to make pretty patchwork patterns and elegant window treatments. Adding quilted texture to bedspreads and coverlets is explained, and the art of making stylish loose slipcovers is demystified.

This section also offers lots of ideas that you can adapt to suit your own requirements. They have been devised to give you the confidence to start designing your own home-decorating projects. For easy reference, the techniques are listed in the same order as they appear in the book.

You already know some of the basics for combining colors, but by now you will be aware that pattern and texture are equally important to successful home-decorating schemes.

HOW TO MAKE PIPING

1. Piece bias fabric strips to make piping for a headboard.
2. Wrap fabric around cording, right side out and raw edges even.
3. Using a zipper foot, stitch close to cording.
4. Place piping against edge of batting and staple piping to headboard within piping seam allowance.

Mix and match fabrics to create a sense of movement and texture across the surface of your quilt.

LAYERING A QUILT

1. A quilt is made up of 3 basic layers. Layer them on a flat surface—first the backing fabric, right side down; then the batting; and finally the top fabric, right side up.
2. Either baste with thread or use large safety pins to hold the layers together until quilting is complete.

HOW TO SEW A QUILT

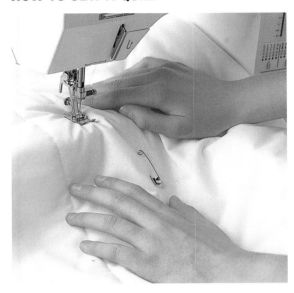

1. When machine sewing, be sure large items are well supported to prevent the fabric and stitches from distorting.
2. Roll up the excess fabric and secure it with safety pins while sewing.
3. Support the item on the work surface or a chair behind the machine and on your knees in front.

A patchwork coverlet or quilt is the perfect way to experiment with different patterns and colors. Above, the plain fabrics create an effective foil for the pretty floral pattern.

HOW TO MITER A BORDER

1. Along each short end of borders, mark 2 in. (5 cm) in from long edge.
2. With one border end flat, fold adjacent border under at a 45° angle; lay over flat border so marks meet and miter is formed.
3. Fold and pin in place.

HOW TO MAKE A DOUBLE-FOLD BIAS BINDING

1. To make bias binding, cut fabric strips on the bias, 4 times the finished width.
2. For right length, sew together strips at a 45° angle. Press in half, wrong sides facing.
3. Open the binding out flat. Press one raw edge to the center fold.
4. Press other raw edge ⅛ in. (3 mm) from the center fold. Refold and press.

Instead of an ordinary throw pillow, you can make a round bolster with beautiful fabric and decorate it with welting, a button, or a tassel.

HOW TO MAKE PERFECT PATCHWORK

1. The most fundamental trick to creating perfect patchwork is to cut the fabric accurately.
2. Using a rotary cutter on a cutting mat will help you do just that.
3. Always run the cutter up the side of a quilter's ruler, always away from you, and keep your fingers out of the way.

INSERTING A ZIPPER

1. To insert a zipper, press seam and opening.
2. Open zipper. With right sides facing, pin and stitch one side of the zipper along one fold of the opening, using a zipper foot.
3. Close zipper. On the right side, pin opening closed and sew around the remaining side and bottom edges.

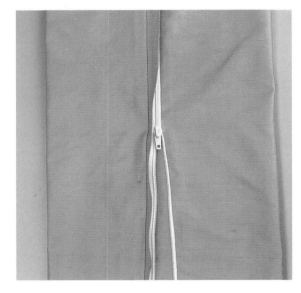

PIN WELTING

1. Pin welting around the fabric, aligning the raw edges.
2. Using a zipper foot, sew the welting close to the cord. Overlap the folded ends where two ends meet.
3. Pin, baste, and sew the second panel of fabric to the first, right sides facing. Trim the seam allowance and turn out.

CREATIVE THINKING

The projects in this section will give you lots of ideas for using fabrics, trimmings, and your sewing skills creatively. Think about changing the fibers, colors, and patterns to suit your own needs. It's only a short leap to designing your own, so here are a few more ideas to inspire you.

- Complement opulent silks in fabulous bold colors with really extravagent tassels, cords, and braids. The more the colors clash, the more exotic the effect.

- Try sewing quilted lines on subtly textured plain fabrics to give sophisticated interest. Sometimes the simplest designs are the most effective: Try, for example, simple, evenly spaced diagonals on a slubby silk.

- Use hand embroidery or fabric paint to add charm to your projects. You could randomly scatter delicate sprigs of leaves or flowers over a transparent drape.

- Machine embroidery is another way of adding embellishment. Simple automatic stitches can produce stunning effects. For example, choose a stitch that contrasts little splashes of colored thread with thinner lines. Work this stitch in matte or shiny thread in one single line to pick out a seam or repeated to create a fabulous texture.

MEASURING FOR CURTAINS

- Measure the curtain track or rod, including any overlap. Decide how full you want the curtains to be—for example, twice the amount of fabric will give very full curtains. Multiply the two figures to give the full curtain width.

- Divide the curtain width by the fabric width to give the number of widths needed. If this gives an odd number and you need two curtains, cut one width up the middle and attach one piece to the outside edge of each curtain.

- Measure the drop of the curtain, taking into consideration where the top will sit in relation to the track or rod and adding an allowance for the top turning and the bottom hem. Add the length of any pattern repeat.

- Multiply total curtain drop by the number of widths needed. Subtract the length of just one pattern repeat if included. This final figure gives you the total fabric requirement.

PATTERN AND TEXTURE

Different scales of pattern have different effects, so choose the appropriate one for the space that the project will occupy. Plain fabrics also make a useful contribution to a scheme by giving any patterned fabrics space to breathe.

- Big bold patterns are dramatic, but they tend to dominate. Choose them for large areas such as curtains and bedspreads, where they can be shown off to the best possible advantage.

- Small patterns are more subtle. They tend to merge with similar neighboring patterns and can seem to disappear from a distance. They are best on smaller items such as pillows and place mats.

- To give the whole scheme a feeling of balance, whether in a room or on a patchwork quilt, combine small-, medium-, and large-scale patterns.

- It is just as important to mix textures to create interest. Glamorous, shiny fabrics can seem cold on their own, while rough textures and piles will add a relaxed, rich feel that is more satisfyingly subtle.

Fabric Headboards

A softly padded fabric-covered headboard brings comfort and style to any bedroom.

A headboard is fundamental to creating a well-dressed bed. Rather than spend a small fortune on a purchased headboard, make a simple one from plywood cut to the desired size and shape, and cover it with batting and fabric.

To design the headboard, make a template from heavy paper and hang it at the head of the bed. Adjust the size and shape until you are satisfied that it suits both the bed and the room.

Splurge on two fabulous-looking coordinating fabrics that pick up the colors from the walls or bed linens already used in the room.

Making a padded fabric headboard with a shirred border provides an opportunity to introduce complementary patterns and colors to a room. For a decorator look, try mixing small prints with stripes or plaids, large prints with smaller ones, or lush florals with solids.

One of the simplest headboard shapes to make is the curved rectangle shown here. In order to ensure that a headboard suits both bed and room, draw the desired size and shape on paper and hang it at the head of the bed.

Once the size and shape of the headboard is perfected on paper, have a lumberyard cut the shape or transfer the outline onto ⅝-in. (15-mm) plywood and cut it yourself using a cross-cut saw or jigsaw.

Cutting Fabric and Batting

Choose medium-weight fabrics with a fairly tight weave. Use marked plywood headboard as pattern.

- From main fabric, cut front and back pieces equal to inner section plus 3 in. (7.5 cm) all around.
- From contrast fabric, cut three border strips 9 in. (23 cm) wide by length of marked border line x 3. Piece strips as needed.
- From high-loft batting, cut shaped piece equal to inner section and 8 in. (20 cm)-wide strips for covering border area.
- Cut enough 2 in. (5 cm)-wide bias fabric strips to cover length of cording equal to length of curved border placement line, or use purchased piping.

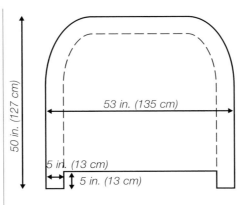

53 in. (135 cm)
50 in. (127 cm)
5 in. (13 cm)
5 in. (13 cm)

1 Following this headboard diagram for standard double bed, cut out headboard shape from plywood, including bottom legs. Measure and mark 5 in. (13 cm) from top and side cut edges to indicate inner edge of border. Draw border line.

3 Place main fabric over batting, with edges 1½ in. (4 cm) beyond batting. Beginning at top, staple fabric to plywood every 1 in. (2.5 cm), pulling fabric taut. Continue stapling down sides, alternating sides every few staples. Pull lower edge to back and staple.

5 Join border strips to achieve desired length. Baste two rows of stitches along one long side, first 1 in. (2.5 cm) from cut edge, then ¼ in. (5 mm) away from first row of stitches. Pull threads to evenly gather fabric to fit around inner curve.

2 Using marked border line on headboard for shape, cut batting and fabrics as instructed in guidelines. Beginning at bottom edge, apply craft glue over entire center section of headboard; glue on batting. Let glue dry completely.

4 Piece bias fabric strips to make piping. Wrap fabric around cording, right side out and raw edges even. Using zipper foot, stitch close to cording. Place piping against edge of batting and staple piping to headboard within piping seam allowance.

6 Place gathered piece facedown over headboard, with basting stitches over previous staples; starting at top, staple border inside basting stitches, close to piping, adjusting gathers as needed. Alternate stapling down each side.

7 Glue batting strips to border of headboard, covering raw edge of gathered fabric. Batting pieces should butt close to each other. At curves, flatten batting to ease in fullness. Wrap batting to wrong side of headboard and glue.

8 Starting at center of top edge and working down sides, pull fabric border over batting to wrong side of headboard. Keeping gathers even and fabric taut, form small tucks on wrong side. Staple fabric in place.

9 Fold raw edges of back fabric under 1–2 in. (2.5–5 cm). Apply craft glue to uncovered areas on back. Place fabric over back and smooth out. Using glue gun, secure backing over edge of fabric border. Drill holes in legs and bolt to bed-frame braces.

TRY THIS!

For an elegant, tailored headboard, eliminate the shirred border and cut the plywood into an interesting shape. Glue padding to the entire front of the headboard. Cut the front fabric 4 in. (10 cm) larger all around than the plywood. Stretch the fabric over the batting and staple it to the back of the headboard, clipping into corners to ease. Cut the back fabric the same size as the plywood and fold all edges under 1 in. (2.5 cm). Glue the back fabric over the raw edges of the front fabric. Glue decorative cording along the edge.

Making a Headboard Cover

There are other types of interesting headboards you can choose if you don't want a padded one. For a quick change of decor, make a simple tie on cover to slip on and off at whim over an existing headboard. Make several covers to match or complement your bed linens. These removable headboard covers can be tossed into the washing machine for easy care. To obtain muted stripes as shown here, use the wrong side of the fabric on the outside.

To make the headboard cover, you need enough medium- to heavy-weight fabric to cut a piece equal to the width of the headboard plus 8 in. (20 cm) for hems plus 4 in. (10 cm) for ease by 2 x (length of headboard plus 4 in./10 cm) plus thickness of headboard. If fabric panels must be joined to obtain the desired width, cut two panels to the required length; cut one in half lengthwise and join to the sides of the second panel; then cut out the cover piece. Use 1 in. (2.5 cm) grommets and rawhide thongs for lacing.

Dress up a bed set with a removable laced fabric cover slipped over an existing headboard. This Americana-inspired navy-and-white striped denim headboard cover gives this otherwise basic bed a finished, contemporary look.

1 Press and sew 1-in. (2.5-cm) double hem to wrong side of cover (wrong side of fabric is cover's right side) along top and bottom edges. Sew 2 in. (5 cm)-wide double hem on sides.

2 Mark center of cover sides, 1 in. (2.5 cm) from edge; mark placement for first grommets 2 in. (5 cm) from either side of center, then mark every 4 in. (10 cm) so grommets line up when cover is folded in half. Apply grommets at markings.

3 Slip cover over headboard and align grommets. Insert end of one thong through first grommets to back and knot. Lace free end though grommets around sides, from back to front. Repeat opposite side. Knot end.

Quick and Easy Quilted Bedspreads

Make a cozy bedspread by sandwiching batting between two layers of fabric and anchoring them together with decorative machine-stitched quilting.

Thanks to sewing machines, quilting is no longer the painstaking process it used to be. Today's quilters can simply create luxurious pieces to bring warmth and also beauty to their homes in just a weekend.

More than a money-saver, making your own bedspread lets you custom-match fabrics to your bed linens or bedroom furnishings. The eggshell comforter shown is machine-quilted with an allover "apple-core" pattern; parallel quilting lines form the wide border around the quilt.

The apple-core pattern is formed by machine quilting easy-to-follow continuous lines. Use the same pattern in the center of a small crib quilt to make a soft wrap for a baby.

Make the pattern by drawing a circle with a 2-in. (5-cm) radius on paper. Fold the circle in half twice and draw a line along each fold. Draw an arc, also with a 2-in. (5-cm) radius from the end of one line to the end of the one next to it. Repeat on the opposite side. Trace the outline onto clear acetate.

A closely woven cotton or polyester/cotton blend in a solid color shows the quilting pattern best. Fabric with a slight sheen or texture can also be used.

Baste the quilt layers together with safety pins. Machine-quilt with 100% cotton, cotton-wrapped polyester, or quilting thread.

Fabric-cutting Guidelines

Use a medium- to low-loft polyester batting for machine quilting.

- For top of 83 x 62 in. (2.1 x 1.57 m) finished bedspread, cut one 50 x 37 in. (127 x 94 cm) center panel; cut two 13½ x 50 in. (34 x 127 cm) and two 17½ x 62 in. (44 x 157 cm) border strips. After marking grid on center panel, sew short border strips to sides of panel, then sew long border strips to top and bottom to form bedspread top.
- Cut two 83-in. (2.1-m) lengths for bedspread back; join to form 83 x 62 in. (2.1 x 1.57 m) piece.
- Trim batting to extend 2 in. (5 cm) beyond backing on all sides.
- Attach walking foot to sewing machine to help feed layers evenly through while quilting.

You'll Need:

- ✓ 8¼ yd. (7.54m) 54 in. (1.37-m)-wide fabric
- ✓ Polyester batting
- ✓ White cotton or quilting thread
- ✓ Water-soluble disappearing marker
- ✓ Clear acetate, fine-tipped permanent marker & craft knife
- ✓ Scissors, ruler, tape measure, safety pins, & straight pins
- ✓ Pair of compasses
- ✓ Sewing machine with quilting foot (walking foot/even-feed foot).

1 Wash and press fabrics before cutting pieces. Cut away selvages from backing lengths and sew two long pieces together with ½-in. (1-cm) seam. Keeping seam centered, trim backing to 62-in. (1.57-m) width. Press seam open.

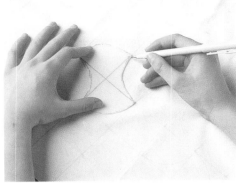

2 Mark center panel with 2 in. (5 cm)-square grid. Trace apple-core shape from pattern sheet directly onto clear acetate; cut out template with craft knife. Place template on grid as shown and draw around it with disappearing marker.

3 With ½-in. (1-cm) seams, join side borders to sides of center panel, then join larger borders across top and bottom. Finger press seams open. Do not press with iron, which could set marker dye.

4 Place batting on top of backing fabric. Place quilt top faceup over batting; smooth out. Using safety pins, pin layers together, beginning at center and working outward. Pin around outer edge.

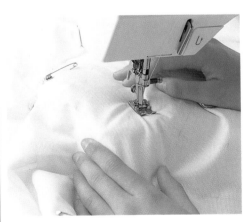

5 Begin quilting center panel at one corner; take one small backstitch, then use medium-length stitch to follow curved apple-core lines diagonally across panel. Continue stitching parallel undulating lines across top.

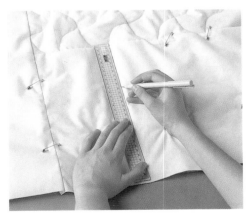

6 Stitch continuous apple-core lines going in opposite diagonal. When apple-core quilting is finished, begin marking side borders with straight lines for quilting. Mark at 2-in. (5-cm) intervals to line up with grid used to mark center panel.

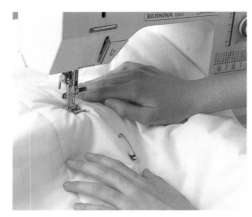

7 Begin quilting straight lines at one side, making sure there are no puckers underneath. Do not let bedspread hang down or the weight will pull fabric and distort stitches. Roll up excess fabric while sewing.

8 Cut four (3½ in./9 cm-wide) binding strips across fabric width to equal each side of spread. Press lengthwise in half, wrong sides together. Pin to top with edges even. Sew binding, starting and stopping ¾ in. (2 cm) from ends.

9 Fold binding to back of quilt, mitering at corners and encasing raw edges. Slipstitch to seam line on back, making sure stitches do not show on top side.

Crafter's Corner

Keep the leftover pieces of batting to make pillows or soft toys. Small pieces of batting can be teased out and used to stuff small dolls or toys. Quilt batting can also be used to make pillow inserts or to add a soft padding to appliqués.

Consider using extra-wide fabric or cotton sheeting to avoid having a seam on the back of the bedspread.

TRY THIS!

A ruffle gives a soft, feminine look to a quilted bedspread and can also serve the practical purpose of lengthening a spread to fit a larger bed. A ruffle can be attached to an already finished bedspread with hook-and-loop fastener tape, which also lets you remove it and change it to suit your mood or the season.

For the ruffle, cut a strip of matching or coordinating fabric to twice the perimeter of the quilt by twice the desired ruffle width plus 1 in. (2.5 cm) for seam allowances. Fold the strip in half and gather along the raw edges. Check the fit of the ruffle and distribute the gathers evenly, then bind the raw edges with bias tape. Attach one half of the fastener tape to the ruffle binding and the corresponding half to the back edges of the bedspread.

Making Quilted Pillows

When buying fabric for your quilt, make sure to purchase some extra to make matching pillows. You will need a 20-in. (50-cm) length of fabric for each cushion, plus a 13-in. (33-cm) long zipper, batting for the front of the pillow, and a 17-in. (43-cm) square pillow insert.

The apple-core quilting pattern works just as well in a square as in a rectangle. Just draw a 2-in. (5-cm) grid as for the bedspread. If you have had no previous experience machine quilting, it may be helpful to make the pillow cover before attempting the bedspread. If you find that the batting gets caught in the sewing machine when you are quilting the pillow top, add a thin backing of cheesecloth.

The pillow illustrated has a zipper sewn into one side for easy removal of the insert. However, you may simply stitch the opening closed with a fine slipstitch, use snaps, or divide the back into two overlapping hemmed sections that you fasten with buttons.

Always choose a machine-washable fabric so your pillows can be kept clean and fresh, even if you take them along on a picnic.

1 Cut two (18-in./46-cm) squares for each pillow. Using disappearing marker and ruler, draw 14-in. (35-cm) square centered on top piece; mark with 2-in. (5-cm) square grid and quilting pattern. Pin top piece to batting and machine quilt.

2 Place pillow top and bottom pieces together, right sides together. Along one side seam, pin and stitch 2½ in. (6 cm) at top and bottom of seam, leaving 13-in. (33-cm) zipper opening at center. Follow instructions in zipper package to sew in new zipper.

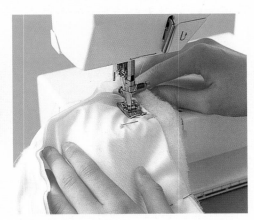

3 Open zipper. With right sides together, stitch three remaining sides with ½-in. (1-cm) seams. Turn pillow cover right side out. Put pillow form inside cover and close zipper.

Gift Bags for Special Occasions

Wrap a present—no matter the size—in a pretty, reusable fabric bag and give a gift-within-a-gift. Plain or fancy, elegant or homespun, gift bags are unique.

Use a holiday plaid to sew up a simple drawstring bag appliquéd with felt evergreen trees.

Made any size, fabric gift bags make wrapping oddly shaped or simple-to-guess gifts. They are also useful for storing jewelry, scarves, cosmetics, hosiery, and many other items.

Use tightly woven fabrics that can support the gift inside, such as velvet, satin, taffeta, brocade, damask, and silk. Because the lining is visible in these shaped-top bags, be sure the chosen fabric complements the main fabric. Use pretty ribbons or cords strung with small decorations to keep the bags closed.

The shaped bags shown are about 14 in. (35 cm) long, but you can lengthen or shorten them as desired. Make a paper pattern for the shaped top edge. Draw a 12-in. (30-cm) line. Divide it into equal intervals and create a repeating pattern of equal triangles, curves, or crenellations. Cut out.

These bags are very easy to make; it is the choice of fabric, pull cords, and trims that give them character, while the shaped opening forms a designer-style collar to show off a decorative lining.

Guidelines for Sewing Corners

These sewing tips will help achieve perfectly squared corners and V-shaped points.

- When stitching points or corners, set stitch length to 15–20 stitches per inch and sew for 2 in. (5 cm) on adjacent sides of corners and points; trim across corner seam allowances.
- Use point turner or pencil with dull point to push out corners after turning bag right side out.

You'll Need:

✓ Paper, pencil & scissors

✓ Straight & safety pins

✓ Fabric marking pen

✓ Sewing machine with buttonhole attachment

✓ Hand-sewing needle & thread

✓ Iron

✓ Point turner & seam ripper

For 14-in. (35-cm) lined bag:

✓ Fabrics: ½ yd. (45 cm) each velvet & lining fabric

✓ 1 yd. (90 cm) ribbon

✓ Small ball ornaments

For appliquéd bag:

✓ 1 yd. (90 cm) plaid broadcloth

✓ 1 yd. (90 cm) ¾ in. (2 cm)-wide ribbon

✓ Fusible web

✓ Green felt

1 Place the right sides of the fabric together. Mark a 13 x 15 in. (33 x 38 cm) rectangle on back. Centrally across one short edge, mark out your pattern for the shaped top. Add ½-in. (1-cm) seam allowance around top and sides of the pattern. Cut out two pieces. Cut out two more pieces from lining.

3 Press all seams open. On each section, with right sides together, align seams at each corner and pin. Mark stitching line perpendicular to seams and 3 in. (7.5 cm) in from corner. Stitch; do not trim.

5 Turn bag right side out, pull out corners. Sew lining opening closed by hand. To form the casing, sew two parallel lines of running stitch, one 1½ in. (4 cm) below the bottom of the shaped pattern, and the next ¾ in. (2 cm) below the first. Sew two ½-in. (1-cm) buttonholes across the casing, 1 in. (2.5 cm) apart and midway between the side seams.

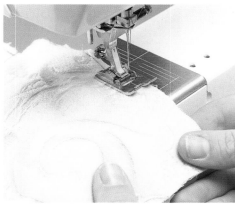

2 With right sides facing, pin lining together. Stitch down one side, across bottom, leaving a 4-in. (10-cm) opening for turning, then up remaining side. Sew velvet pieces, right sides together, along sides and entire bottom.

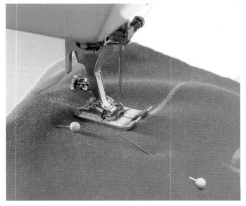

4 Slide lining inside velvet bag with right sides together. Pin sections together along top edge. Stitch around top of bag, following marking and pivoting at corners; trim close to stitching.

6 Using seam ripper, carefully open buttonholes. Attach safety pin to end of ribbon. Insert into one buttonhole; thread through casing and out other buttonhole. Insert and glue ribbon ends into ball ornaments without hanger tops.

Making an Appliquéd Gift Bag

1 Iron fusible web onto felt. Transfer tree template onto paper backing. Cut out four trees to go on front of bag. Cut out two more trees without fusible web. Cut two 22 x 30 in. (55 x 76 cm) plaid pieces for bag.

2 Iron fuse-backed trees to one bag piece. Add decorative stitching down center of tree. With right sides of bag together, stitch down one side, along bottom, and up second side, stopping 4½ in. (12 cm) from top.

3 Press top edge under ½ in. (1 cm). Fold top over 2 in. (5 cm). Stitch close to inside folded edge and again ¾ in. (2 cm) above. Thread ribbon through casing at opening. Stitch down center of tree tassels to ends of ribbon.

TRY THIS!

Whether you have run out of wrapping paper or are just looking for an exciting new way to wrap a gift, look to kitchen linens. The colorful patterns found on many kitchen towels make them a festive and practical form of gift wrap.

Roll or wrap the gift, in much the same way as candy is wrapped with paper. Fashion the loose ends of the towels into one or two bunches or folded flaps and tie with raffia, ribbon, or any decorative cord. Insert dried flowers, sprays of wheat, or pinecones into the bow to trim.

Making a Christmas Santa Bag

The gift-laden Christmas season is full of wrapping, storing, and transporting challenges. A large, cheerful gift bag, just like Santa's, is the solution.

One yard (90 cm) of a holiday-inspired solid for the outer bag and the same amount of a festive print for the lining will make the Santa bag pictured. Enlarge the gingerbread men shapes for the appliqué from the photograph. Cut out the shapes from a 24 x 30 in. (60 x 76 cm) piece of tan fabric, then fuse it to the outer bag. Trim and button details are added.

The outside is decorated first, then the side and bottom seams of both the outside and lining pieces are sewn. A 4-in. (10-cm) opening is left along the bottom edge of the lining for turning. The lining is sewn to the outer fabric along the top edge, leaving two ½-in. (1-cm) openings, about 2 in. (5 cm) apart. After turning the bag right side out, a casing is formed by stitching around the bag 1 in. (2.5 cm) from the top edge. A shiny twisted cord is threaded through the openings.

A large holiday Santa bag is useful to transport gifts to relatives or to school or to hide small gifts away from the eyes of inquisitive family members. It is also great for storing Christmas decorations.

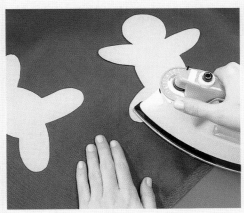

1 Iron fusible web onto tan fabric. Trace four gingerbread men onto fabric; cut out shapes. Plan placement of gingerbread men, remove backing from web, and fuse in place.

2 Using fabric glue, attach rickrack to gingerbread men as shown. Sew buttons on for eyes and front trim and place them randomly around bag. Use fabric paint to draw smiles and to mimic blanket stitches around appliqué edges.

3 Sew separate outer sack and lining, leaving opening on lining bottom. With right sides facing, sew bags together along top edge, leaving two ½-in. (1-cm) openings 2 in. (5 cm) apart; turn right side out. Stitch casing and insert cord; knot cord ends.

Stylish Place Mats

Napkin rings sewn to place mats—what could be more ingenious! Not only delightful to look at, these all-in-one combos make setting any table a breeze.

With this easy-to-sew place mat/napkin ring combo, a pretty and unified place setting is always guaranteed. Since the rings are attached to the mats, you need not worry about any lost pieces. And just rotating the mat puts the napkin on either the right or the left side.

Make the combo out of two coordinating fabrics, such as these charming green-and-beige checks and florals. Pretty wooden buttons and matching green ribbon trim provide the finishing touches.

The size of the place mat and the position and orientation of the napkin rings can be altered easily. For place mats without an inner ribbon border, sew the napkin ring 1–2 in. (2.5–5 cm) from the side edge. If you prefer, follow the tab ring instructions to sew separate buttoned napkin rings to match place mats you already own.

This combination place mat and napkin ring is sewn from two coordinating fabrics with a solid-colored ribbon for accent. Cut the back piece, center, and the napkin ring from one fabric, and the place mat front (which becomes a border) from the remaining fabric.

Only one button is needed for each place setting, so purchase fine-quality buttons that blend perfectly with the style and character of the fabrics.

Sewing Guidelines

Look for fabric with a soil- and stain-resistant finish so the mats will stay fresh looking. To add loft to the mat, fuse a layer of fleece to the front piece and fusible interfacing to the back piece.

- For 12 x 17 in. (30 x 43 cm) finished place mat size, cut 13 x 18 in. (33 x 46 cm) rectangle from fabric selected for place mat front and from fusible interfacing and fusible fleece. From coordinating fabric, cut 13 x 18 in. (33 x 46 cm) piece for place mat back, 8 x 11 in. (20 x 28 cm) piece for center section, and 4½-in. (12-cm) square for napkin ring. Cut another 4½-in. (12-cm) square from fusible interfacing as well. All dimensions include ½-in. (1-cm) seam allowances.
- Pin matching ribbon over edges of center section and topstitch along both edges of ribbon.
- If desired, use ruler and pencil to draw pointed end on napkin ring to use as guideline.

You'll Need:

✓ ½ yd. (45 cm) each of coordinating fabrics

✓ Fusible fleece & fusible interfacing

✓ 1¼ yd. (1.15 m) matching ribbon

✓ ¾-in. (2-cm) button

✓ Sewing needle & thread, tape measure, straight pins, & scissors

✓ Sewing machine with buttonhole attachment

✓ Iron

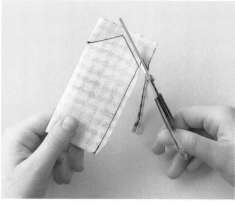

1 Cut out all fabric pieces. Follow package instructions to fuse interfacing to wrong side of napkin ring square. Fold fabric in half, right sides facing. Stitch long, open edge and sew point at one short end. Trim excess fabric; turn right side out.

2 Press napkin ring seams flat, so point and seams are sharp. Using your sewing machine's built-in buttonhole stitch setting, make buttonhole about ½ in. (1 cm) from napkin ring's pointed end. Carefully cut buttonhole open with scissors or seam ripper.

3 Follow manufacturer's instructions to fuse fleece to wrong side of front and interfacing to wrong side of back. Zigzag stitch smaller rectangle to center of mat front. Pin ribbon over zigzagged edges. Stitch along both edges of ribbon.

4 Pin napkin ring to center of one short side of mat front with raw edges even. Pin front and back pieces together, right sides together. Stitch ½ in. (1 cm) from edges, catching end of tab in stitching; leave 4-in. (10-cm) opening along one edge for turning.

5 Trim excess fabric diagonally at corners. Turn place mat right side out and poke out all corners. Machine or hand stitch opening closed. Press place mat flat.

6 Mark button placement along center of ribbon border on napkin ring edge. Hand sew button in place.

Quilted Place Mats

Reversible place mats made with coordinating fabrics are ideal for livening up a table setting.

When you need a quick dress-up for the table, especially for more informal dining occasions, use these reversible place mats made from colorful printed fabrics. A padding of fusible fleece plus machine quilting adds a soft look while providing protection for your table surface from hot plates.

You can get exquisite results by combining identical prints in various different colors, using one for each side, and then another for the border. Coordinate the fabrics with other kitchen or dining-room accessories, such as pretty window valances and curtains and chair pads.

For another look, round off the corners of the place mats and trim the edges with a ruffle or a neat bias binding. For additional texture and interest, quilt the place mats with a diamond pattern.

Create two place mats in one by using contrasting colored fabrics on two sides. Quilt both pieces separately, then join them with a binding that is mitered at the corners.

Place Mat Guidelines

The place mat shown has a finished size of 12 x 18 in. (30 x 46 cm). However, you can make your place mats smaller or larger as desired.

- When using large prints, center and align motifs.
- Fusible fleece provides cushioning for fabric. Adhere to fabric following manufacturer's instructions. To simplify quilting, use fusible fleece with premarked quilting lines.
- Select diagonal stripe or diamond quilting pattern. Mark wrong side with pencil and ruler, keeping lines parallel.
- Use quilting guide if one is available for your machine.

You'll Need:

- ✓ Fabrics for 2 place mats: ½ yd. (45 cm) fabric in 2 colors; ¼ yd. (23 cm) contrasting fabric for borders
- ✓ ½ yd. (45 cm) fusible fleece
- ✓ Pencil & ruler; scissors
- ✓ Sewing needle; straight pins
- ✓ Sewing machine & thread

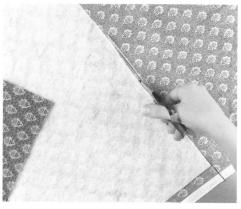

1 For each place mat, cut two 12 x 18-in. (30 x 46-cm) rectangles, each from a different colored fabric. Cut two pieces fusible fleece to same size.

2 Following manufacturer's instructions, fuse fleece to wrong side of each piece. With pencil and ruler, mark diagonal quilting lines on fusible fleece 2 in. (5 cm) apart, keeping lines parallel.

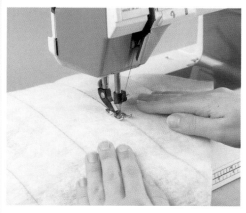

3 Before quilting, test on scrap fabric. Adjust thread tension so stitches are even on top and bottom and fabric is not pulling. Stitch along marked quilting lines on both pieces.

4 Cut four borders from contrasting fabrics: two 4 x 12 in. (10 x 30 cm) and two 4 x 18 in. (10 x 46 cm). With right sides together, pin one short border to one short mat edge, 1 in. (2.5 cm) in from mat edge; stitch with ½-in. (1-cm) seams beginning and ending 1½ in. (4 cm) in from end. Secure thread ends.

5 Press first border open. Stitch long border on in same manner, beginning stitching close to last stitch on previous border. Stitch remaining long and short borders in place in same manner, pressing all borders open.

6 Along each short end of borders, mark 2 in. (5 cm) in from long edge. With one border end flat, fold adjacent border under at a 45° angle, lay over flat border so marks meet and miter is formed. Fold and pin in place.

7 With needle and thread, slipstitch miters together to marked lines. Do not secure thread. Repeat for all corners. Press raw edges of border under ½ in. (1 cm).

8 Press borders 1½ in. (4 cm) to back of mat, encasing raw edges of place mat. Miter corners same as for front, lapping folded corner over flat corner. Complete slipstitching corners. Slipstitch along folded border edge around mat.

Crafter's Corner

Look for fabrics that are finished with a liquid repellent and a soil-and-stain release. If the fabric you've chosen is unfinished, you can treat the fabric yourself by using a stain-resistant spray. Select color-fast fabrics that are easy to care for so your place mat will retain its crisp appearance after laundering.

TRY THIS!

You can make small basket liners using a similar method of construction. Make a pattern by placing paper in a basket and tracing the base; round off the corners. Quilt two bases as for the place mats. Cut a continuous strip of ruffle fabric twice the diameter of the basket and twice the desired basket depth plus seam allowances. Sew the short ends to make a loop, then press in half. Gather raw edges to fit around the base. Sew to edges of one base; press seams to wrong side. Press the seam allowances under on the second base, and pin to ruffled half, wrong sides facing. Slipstitch bases together.

Making Napkins and Rings

Fabric napkins are affordable to make and can be designed specifically to suit your needs and to match both your table linens and dinnerware. Choose solid-colored or discreetly patterned fabrics that coordinate with place mats or a tablecloth.

Keep in mind that napkins look best when made from fabrics that can be reversed. Try textured cotton or linen for body and durability. Make dinner-sized napkins about 20 in. (50 cm) square, and finish the edges with a decorative binding cut on the bias from a coordinating fabric.

As a special touch, make matching napkin rings. Cut a 3 x 8 in. (7.5 x 20 cm) strip of fabric and fold in half lengthwise, then stitch along long edges. Turn right side out, then press one end ¼ in. (5 mm) to the inside. Slip the other end inside, and slipstitch together to make a ring. Cut a 2 x 10 in. (5 x 25 cm) strip from the same fabric for the bow. Fold in half, trim the ends diagonally, then sew, leaving an opening in the center of the long side. Turn, stitch the opening closed, and press. Tie around the ring in a decorative bow, then simply fold a napkin and slip it into the ring.

To make your guests feel especially welcome, set the table with beautiful fabric napkins placed in matching napkin rings. It's a simple way to give your table a festive and inviting atmosphere.

1 To fold napkin for napkin ring, lay opened napkin on flat surface. Fold in half diagonally with fold at bottom. Fold two side corners in to meet at center, slightly overlapping. Starting at fold, neatly and evenly roll up napkin.

2 Make sure ends are straight and napkin is of even thickness. Slip napkin ring over rolled napkin, keeping napkin roll intact. Position bow at corner point of rolled up napkin.

Curtains with Contrasting Detail

Make a personal style statement when you're decorating your windows. Choose a mix of colors and fabrics to sew curtains that feature bias-bound edges.

Be your own designer in making any of the curtain designs shown here. Combine favorite styles of large and small prints, contrasting solids, or mix prints with plaids and stripes. Then, to complete your design, select a fabric for the bias binding that matches or contrasts with the curtains' fabrics. For a time-saving way to bind the curtains and tiebacks, purchase a ready-made ¼-in. (5-mm) double-fold bias binding in a complementary color. Prepackaged bindings are sold in 4-yd. (3.65-m) packages in fabric stores.

Begin your creative experience by selecting fabrics for the curtains, including popular prints with romantic flowers, boughs of fruit, ethnic geometric shapes, and classic country looks. For all the designs shown, select soft to crisp fabrics in medium to light weights.

Before purchasing fabrics for curtains, select a curtain rod that is appropriate for a curtain with a casing. Install the rod, then decide on the length of the curtain (from the bottom of the rod to the sill or to the floor), the depth of the heading, which extends above the rod, and the number of panels (widths of fabric) that will be needed.

For opaque fabrics, the full combined curtain widths (including the contrasting center bands) should equal at least twice the window's width. For sheer or lace fabrics, it should be three times the window's width.

Determining Yardage

Use the following formula to determine the cut lengths of the panels and center bands. The cut panels may have to be stitched together.

- Cut length = heading depth (1–3 in. (2.5–7.5 cm) x 2 + ½ in. (1 cm) seam allowance + casing depth (depth of rod plus ¼ in. or 5 mm, ease) x 2 + length from rod to hem + 8 in. (20 cm) for a double hem.
- To determine yardage, multiply cut lengths with number of panels needed.

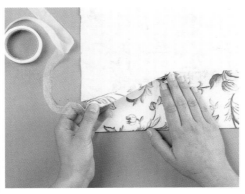

1 If multiple outer panels are needed for width, sew together with ½-in. (1-cm) seams. Form a double hem by pressing 4 in. (10 cm) to wrong side twice. Fuse top of hem in place with fusible tape. If curtain is sheer, edgestitch top of hem in place.

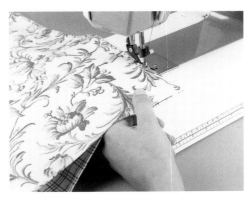

2 Cut center bands to desired widths. Hem in same way as panels. With wrong sides together and hemlines aligned, zigzag one center band to one outer panel along long edges.

3 Open out bias binding. Right sides together, pin narrower seam allowance of binding over one side of zigzag stitches; leave 1 in. (2.5 cm) of binding beyond hem. Stitch binding to curtain along crease line; be sure stitching covers zigzag stitches.

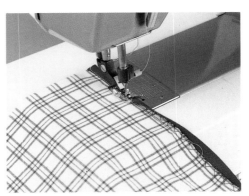

4 Fold end of binding to opposite side of curtain. Refold binding to encase zigzagged edges, then edgestitch along inner edge. Sew a 1-in. (2.5-cm) double hem along outer long edges of outer panels. Encase inner curtain edges with bias binding.

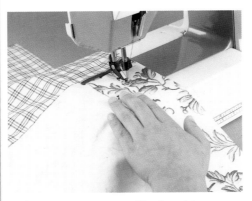

5 At curtain top press ½ in. (1 cm) to wrong side. Measure down to a length equal to desired height of finished casing plus heading plus ¼-in. (5-mm) ease and crease fabric. Edgestitch along lower casing seam, then topstitch upper casing seam.

6 Press finished curtain panels. Remove rod from window and insert rod through curtain casings so contrasting bands hang together in center.

Making Your Own Double-Fold Bias Binding

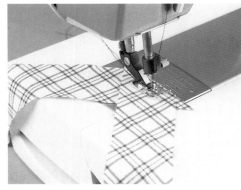

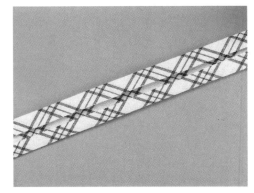

1 Decide on finished width of binding ¼– 1 in. (0.5–2.5cm). Place fabric on top of table or cutting board. Determine true bias (45° angle) across fabric, and draw bias lines that are spaced at a distance equal to four times finished binding width.

2 Cut enough bias strips to equal length of edges to be bound. Right sides together, stitch strip ends together with ¼-in. (5-mm) seam allowances to form desired length; press seams open. Press strip in half, wrong sides together.

3 Open out strip. Press one cut edge to meet at center crease, wrong sides inside. Press opposite edge toward first cut edge, leaving a ⅛-in. (3-mm) gap between cut edges. Refold binding and press. Folded edges should be offset by ⅛ in. (3 mm).

TRY THIS!

When all bias-binding strips are cut across the fabric in the same bias direction, the stripes will angle identically on curtain halves. When half the strips are cut in the opposite diagonal direction, the stripes on both halves will form chevrons.

These cheesecloth curtains have a valance that is cut all-in-one with the body of the curtain. The valance is then pressed toward the front of the curtain. Use fabrics identical on both sides. To cut, determine the length of the curtain, add double the height of the rod plus ¼ in. (5 mm) for easing, and then add 8–15 in. (20–38 cm) for the depth of the valance below the casing. You do not need an allowance for hems or seams. Proportion the valance depth to about one-fourth to one-third the finished curtain length. Finish the edges of the curtain with a 1 in. (2.5 cm)-wide bias binding. To form straight tiebacks, stitch the same binding width with a 1 in. (2.5 cm)-wide seam allowance.

Making Contoured Tiebacks

Shaped tiebacks bound around the edges can enhance any curtain. To determine the correct length of the tieback for your curtains, wrap a tape measure around the hanging curtains and loosen or tighten the tape for the desired appearance. Use the grid art below to make a half-pattern piece, lengthening or shortening the pattern from the fold line to match your measurement. Place the pattern on the fold of fabric to cut a whole tieback piece.

To make a set of tiebacks, you will need to purchase ¼ in.–⅜ in. (5–20 mm)-wide double-fold bias binding, two pairs of ½-in. (1-cm) hook-and-loop fastener circles or squares with adhesive backings, two ½ in. (1 cm)-diameter plastic rings, and two cup hooks for the wall.

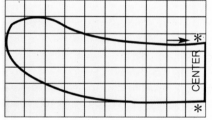

1 square = 1 in. (2.5 cm)
* Lengthen or shorten here
For one pair of tiebacks, cut four from fabric and four from interfacing.

Two colors of ¼-in. (5-mm) gingham check were used for these kitchen curtains, bound with a 1 in. (2.5 cm)-wide yellow binding. For a dramatic effect, combine different check sizes. Just be sure the sizes are noticeably different, such as a 1-in. (2.5-cm) versus a ¼-in. (5-mm) check or a ½-in. (1-cm) versus a ⅛-in. (3-mm) check. Use the same guideline for combining two coordinating fabric prints.

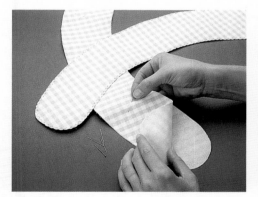

1 Fuse interfacing to wrong side of tieback pieces. Pin wrong sides together and zigzag around cut edges. Open out binding; fold one end ½ in. (1 cm) to wrong side; pin.

2 Right sides together, pin narrow seam allowance of binding over tieback edges; stitch along crease line; overlap binding ends. Refold bias binding to encase edges.

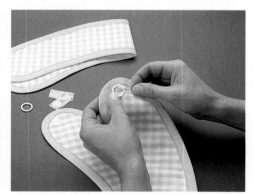

3 Edgestitch inner edge of binding. Attach each half of fastener tape or squares to insides of curved ends. At one curved end of each tieback, sew one ring to back side. Attach hooks to wall.

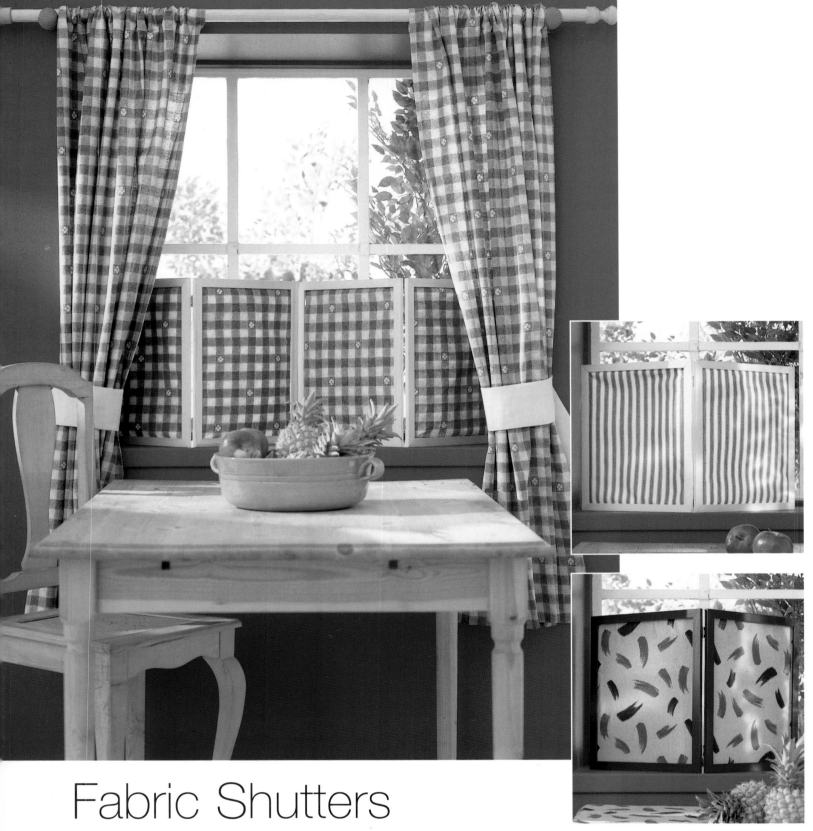

Fabric Shutters

Easy to make from wooden frames and fabric, these colorful shutters provide just the right combination of privacy and light.

To make these shutters, simply attach fabric to the back of wooden picture frames, then hinge the frames together. Open the shutters for maximum privacy or fold them to the sides for more light. Shutters coordinate beautifully with a curtain, as shown here in a pretty flowered check, or with a perky valance.

The doubled fabric panels create an effective light filter and give the shutters a finished look from the outside. Attached by thin strips of hook-and-loop fastener tape, the fabric panels can be removed easily for laundering or a change of decor.

The wooden frames can be painted to coordinate with the fabric or with the color scheme of the room. To prevent an unattractive look when the sun shines through, back irregularly patterned fabrics with a solid fabric. If using a striped, checked, or other evenly repeated pattern, make sure to match the pattern lines on the front and back fabric pieces.

Select the fabrics for the coverlet to blend with the accent colors and style of the room. Cotton fabrics, such as chintz, are ideal for this project. Cotton blends can also be used. Avoid very thick or very thin fabrics.

Use a medium-weight polyester batting for the filling. Large seamless sheets of batting are available in arts and crafts stores and fabric stores.

To quilt, set machine for straight stitching—about 12 stitches per 1 in. (2.5 cm)—and attach a walking foot or quilting foot if you have one.

Coverlet-making Guidelines

Use a sheet in the appropriate size for the backing, or join fabric panels together. Wash and press fabrics before cutting.

- Coverlet is square. To figure size of finished coverlet, measure length of bed and add desired overhang. Adjust overhang if too long at sides. Add ½ in. (1 cm) for seam allowances.
- For 96 in. (2.4 m) square queen-size coverlet shown, cut 36 in. (90-cm) square of floral fabric for center square.
- Surround center square with four borders, the first about 3 in. (7.5 cm) wide, finished, and each additional about 9 in. (23 cm) wide, finished.

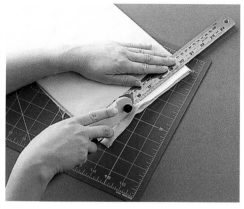

1 Cut 36-in. (90-cm) square for center panel. For first border, fold 16 in. (40 cm) long fabric in half lengthwise, then widthwise, keeping inside folds flat. Using ruler and rotary cutter, trim selvage.

2 Refold fabric and cut equally into four 4 x 44 in. (10 x 110 cm) strips. Fold and cut each remaining border fabric into 10 in. (25 cm)-wide strips; piece strips as needed for desired length on each side of quilt.

3 Center one border strip along one edge of center square, right sides together, raw edges even; leave 4 in. (10 cm) (or width of strip) extending at beginning and end. Stitch together, leaving ½ in. (1 cm) unstitched at ends of center panel. Repeat on other sides.

4 To miter corners, fold corner extensions of border strips back along themselves to wrong side of fabric to make 45° angle. Press fold lines. Repeat at each corner.

5 Fold coverlet diagonally in half, right sides together. Open out pressed corners of strips; match fold lines and stitch along fold lines. Trim seam to ¼ in. (5 mm); press open. Repeat for all four corners.

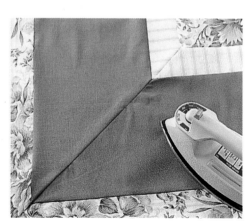

6 Attach remaining borders in same manner, mitering corners on each border. Press seams open.

Quilting the Coverlet

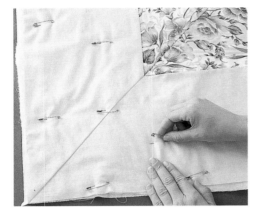

1 Cut sheet or join backing fabric to make 96-in. (2.44-m) square; lay right side down; place batting on top. Smooth wrinkles. Place coverlet top over batting, right side up; use safety pins to hold all layers together.

2 Tightly roll up sides of bedspread; secure with safety pins. Using quilting foot, quilt around motifs in center panel. Quilt in each border seam. Trim backing so edges are even with quilt top.

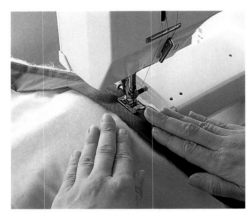

3 Cut enough 3½ in. (9 cm)-wide strips for binding. Join to make one length to go around perimeter. Press binding in half, lengthwise; pin to right side of bedspread, raw edges even. Stitch, mitering corners.

4 Turn binding to back of coverlet. With matching thread, slipstitch folded edge of binding in place by hand, folding mitered corners in place.

TRY THIS!

Make an attractive duvet cover for a comforter. Cut a rectangle of a large-print fabric for the center and use the same method that was used for the coverlet to add borders. Use a bedsheet for the backing, and sew the top and backing together. Purchase snaps or hook-and-loop tape-fastener for the closures.

Change the mood of your bedroom decor by making several duvet covers using different patterns and color schemes. The ethnic print used in the center of this duvet cover will look striking in a colorful, contemporary-styled bedroom.

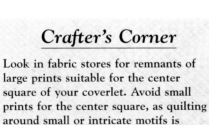

Crafter's Corner

Look in fabric stores for remnants of large prints suitable for the center square of your coverlet. Avoid small prints for the center square, as quilting around small or intricate motifs is difficult.

Buy a ready-made flat sheet to use for the backing of your bed coverlet. This can be cheaper than buying fabric, and the sheet does not need to be pieced to achieve the required size. As standard sizes vary between manufacturers, you may need to open sheet hems to gain a few additional inches.

Bordering a Pillow Cover

Luxurious throw pillows are a plush addition to stylish bed linens and lend themselves to a variety of settings. Use the same steps for making the coverlet top to make a pretty square pillow. Begin with a suitably sized square for the center, then add one or two different-colored borders to achieve the desired size. Square bed pillows and pillow forms are available in a variety of sizes. Or, if you are inclined, give an existing pillow a fresh, new look with a beautifully tailored cover to match your room decor.

Consider using remnants of tone-on-tone fabrics, as shown, or recycle some leftover fabric from your curtains, bedspread, and/or slipcovers for the center, then mix and match others for the borders.

For easy removal of the pillow, make a large opening in the back of the cushion using two overlapping hemmed pieces of fabric that are buttoned together with large, stylish buttons.

A pillow cover with a center panel and complementary borders in neutral tones would look great in an informal, contemporary setting. For a more traditional, formal decor, consider using rich fabrics like damask, tapestry, and velvet.

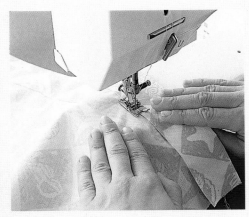

1 For back of cover, cut two pieces, each equal to half of pillow size plus 5 in. (13 cm) extra for center overlap and ½-in. (1-cm) seam allowance on other edges. Press under 2 in. (5 cm) twice along closure edges; blind hem or straight stitch in place.

2 On one back piece, measure and mark three evenly spaced horizontal buttonholes 1 in. (2.5 cm) from folded hem edge. Make buttonholes ⅛ in. (3 mm) larger than diameter of buttons.

3 With right sides together and back pillow pieces overlapping at center, stitch front and back pieces together with ½ in. (1 cm) seams. Turn right side out and press. Sew buttons on right side to correspond with buttonholes.

Cushions with Tufts and Tassels

Transform a hard wooden bench into a comfortable sofa with a custom-made soft cushion that adds a decorative accent to your room.

Sewing a bench cushion is a simple and inexpensive way to turn a wooden bench into a more inviting and comfortable seating area. A pretty fabric cushion, such as the one shown here, accentuates the graceful lines and color of the woodwork. Select a fabric that blends with or accents your decor,

then give the cushions a polished look by tying with tasteful tassels or decorative buttons.

Cushions can be made firm or soft, depending on the foam used. Once you learn the technique, you can make professional-looking cushions for any piece of furniture.

Custom fit the cushion to the specific contours of your bench seat; coordinating tassels tied through the entire depth keep the surface trim and taut. Make a set of throw pillows edged with cording and matching tassels to accent your new bench cushion.

The cushion is made from a layer of foam sandwiched between two sheets of bonded polyester batting. Tassels can be made from yarn or embroidery floss, depending on the look desired.

Sewing Guidelines

For cushions, select closely woven fabrics that will retain their shape after extended use.

- Measure length and width of seat. If seat is square or rectangular, use these dimensions to cut fabric. For seat with unusual contour, such as bow, make paper pattern for entire seat. If sides are straight but corners are cut out, make pattern of corners only.

- Purchase foam at fabric or upholstery stores; they will cut foam for you if you bring along your pattern or dimensions.

- To make tassels, wrap yarn around piece of cardboard of desired length until you reach proper fullness. Slip piece of yarn under top strands and tie securely, then cut yarn at bottom. Make tying strands long enough to thread through cushion for tying on tassels. Tie tassels evenly across cushion cover, alternating spacing from row to row.

You'll Need:

- ✓ Decorator fabric
- ✓ 1 in. (2.5 cm)-thick foam
- ✓ High-loft polyester batting sheets
- ✓ Cotton yarn & 3-in. (7.5-cm) square of cardboard
- ✓ Paper, pencil, tape, permanent marker, scissors & serrated knife or electric knife
- ✓ Silicone lubricant (optional)
- ✓ Sewing machine, needle, & thread
- ✓ Iron

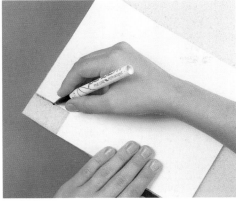

1 Tape sheet of paper over top of seat and trace outline with pencil; cut out pattern. With marker, mark pattern on foam. Use electric or serrated knife to cut foam; if necessary, spray knife with silicone lubricant before cutting.

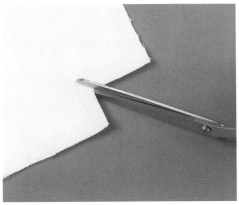

3 With pattern over piece of folded fabric, mark outline, adding ½-in. (1-cm) seam allowance. Cut two pieces for cushion. Clip into corners. Cut 3 in. (7.5 cm)-wide boxing strip to equal cushion circumference plus 1 in. (2.5 cm) for seams; join strips if necessary.

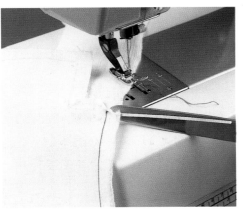

5 Clip into seam allowance of boxing strip at outside corner point. Pin strip around corner, spreading clips on strip and cushion piece; pin until you reach opposite outside corner; clip into strip and continue sewing around corner.

2 Use pattern to cut out two pieces of high-loft batting; sandwich foam between batting pieces so combined thickness equals 2 in. (5 cm). Measure cushion circumference; cut 2 in. (5 cm)-wide batting strip to equal measurement; place around cushion edge.

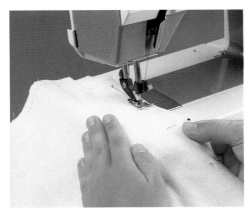

4 Beginning below corner, pin strip along one short side of cushion top with right sides together and edges even. Stitch with ½-in. (1-cm) seam to first outside corner; backstitch.

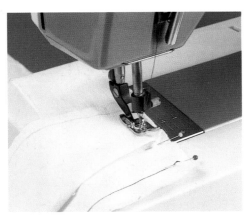

6 Continue in same manner to pin, clip, and stitch boxing strip to cushion piece, clipping corner points at each corner. Join short ends of boxing strip with ½-in. (1-cm) seam. Lightly press corner seams.

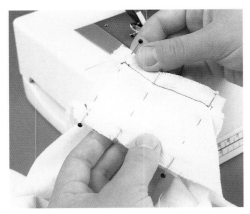  

7 Pin and stitch boxing strip to remaining piece of cover in same manner, leaving opening along one side. Be sure that corners on top and bottom of boxing strip are precisely aligned.

8 Press seams. Turn cover right side out. Insert foam and batting through opening. Be sure to push out all corners so foam snugly fills cover. Slipstich opening closed.

9 Make small tassels. Thread each end of tassel strand onto needle, and thread individually through cushion about ¼ in. (5 mm) apart. Tie yarn ends together on underside of cushion. Tie tassels in even, staggered rows.

Crafter's Corner

To make cushion cover removable for laundering, simply omit the tassels and add a zipper across the back of the cover. Cut one boxing strip to equal the length of the front and both sides. Cut two back boxing strips with lengths equal to the back-edge measurement and widths equal to half the boxing strip height plus seam allowances. Follow the manufacturer's instructions to attach the zipper between the two halves of the back boxing strips. Look for fabric that has a water-resistant and stain-release finish. If necessary, pretreat the fabric with a spray finish designed to safeguard fabrics.

TRY THIS!

Make an attractive wicker patio chair more welcoming with a comfortable fabric cushion. For a fresh look, select a bright floral or fruit pattern to blend with the outdoor setting. Make the cushion from scratch by following the instructions given for the bench cushion. Or refurbish a faded and worn-out cushion with a new fabric cover, and finish the cushion with small, fluffy tassels in a matching color.

Decorating Pillow Edges

Make your sofa more appealing with a beautiful array of soft pillows. Create a lively mix-and-match look by combining different sizes or by mixing solid-colored pillows with a medley of pillows in coordinating patterns.

If the pillows are to be exposed to daily wear, select a firmly woven washable or stain-resistant fabric. The large pillows shown are 20 x 20 in. (50 x 50 cm) and the small pillows are 15 x 15 in. (38 x 38 cm), but you can adjust the size easily. Covers require two pieces of fabric; add ½ in. (1 cm) to all sides for seam allowances. If you prefer to purchase a pillow form to fill your cover, buy it first, measure it to verify the size, and sew the cover to fit.

There are lots of ways to give your pillows extra personality, such as sewing a length of decorative cotton cording around the outside edges or attaching tassels at each corner. To form the tassels, use a thin cotton cord that will fray easily.

Twisted cotton cords, which can be found in a variety of thicknesses and colors, are inexpensive and easy to use to edge pillows. Follow the steps below to form pillow edging and corner tassels with one continuous strand of cord.

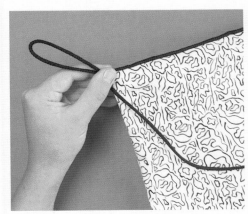

1 Stitch cover pieces with right sides facing, leaving small opening. Turn right side out. Leaving 3-in. (7.5-cm) length free at first corner, slipstitch cording over seam of one edge. At corner, form 3-in. (7.5-cm)-long loop with cord.

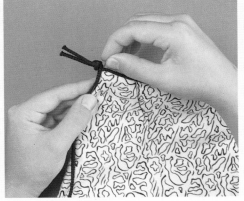

2 At point of corner, tie loop into knot; pull tight. Cut loop at center. Continue in same manner around entire pillow, tying and cutting loops in remaining three corners. When you reach first corner, cut cord 3 in. (7.5 cm) past corner.

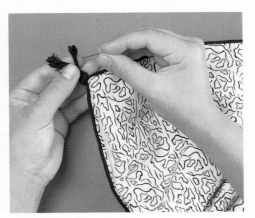

3 Tie beginning and ending 3-in. (7.5-cm) lengths together into final corner knot. With needle, fray ends of cords until tassel is uniform and fluffy. Fray tassels in other corners in same manner. Trim tassels to even length.

Reversible Bedspreads

With a flick of the wrist, you can change the look of your bedroom in as little time as it takes to make up the bed. The secret to the makeover is a reversible bedspread.

A soft bedspread on a newly made bed is a picture of comfort. When you have a reversible spread that matches your room decor regardless of which side is showing, it is also the picture of practicality. Make a light-colored side for summer and a darker side for winter. Or you could use a solid on one side and a print on the other.

A layer of batting between the two fabrics provides stability and warmth to the spread, which can be made in any size, from a baby blanket to a cover for a large bed.

Comfort and color are the keys to selecting bedspread fabrics. Cottons, cotton blends, or synthetics are ideal for their softness and washability. Use complementary or contrasting colors, then finish with a border that works with both sides.

A reversible bedspread usually consists of three layers—the top fabric, contrasting bottom fabric, and a layer of batting in between. Batting is available in a variety of thicknesses at fabric or craft stores. If you are looking for a lighter-weight bedspread, either choose low-loft batting or eliminate the batting altogether.

General Guidelines

Simple measuring, cutting, and straight stitching are all that is required to make this easy reversible bedspread.

- Measure bed to determine size of bedspread. Allow about 12 in. (30 cm) for overhang on each side.
- Cut fabric and batting layers to same size. If necessary, piece fabrics to desired size.
- Add a border of a contrasting color or print for a more finished look.
- To keep layers from shifting, machine-stitch them together at parallel intervals, using small, straight stitches. Use safety pins to hold layers together during sewing.

You'll Need:

- ✓ Fabrics for top, lining, & borders
- ✓ Batting
- ✓ Matching sewing threads
- ✓ Tape measure, ruler, & fabric marking pen
- ✓ Straight pins & scissors
- ✓ Sewing machine
- ✓ Iron & ironing board

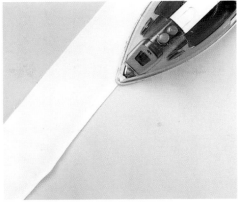

1 Cut lining fabric to finished size of bedspread, adding ½ in. (1 cm) for seams all around; piece fabric as needed. Cut four 4 in. (10 cm)-wide border strips to fit edges of lining. Press under ½ in. (1 cm) along one long edge of each strip.

2 With right sides together, pin long raw edge of one border strip to matching lining edge. Using a ruler, draw right angle at each end of strip to mark sewing line for mitered corner. Repeat for each remaining border strip.

3 Sew adjacent border strips together along diagonal corner lines. Trim these seams to ½ in. (1 cm) and press open. Sew border strips to lining along outer edges, using ½-in. (1-cm) seam and pivoting at corners.

4 Trim corners, turn border to right side, and press. Cut top fabric and batting to finished size, piecing as needed; layer together. Place on wrong side of lining, fabric side up and layered edges tucked under borders. Pin together.

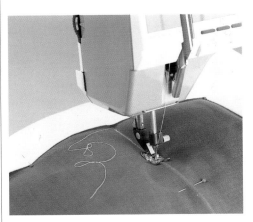

5 Using fabric marker, mark lines for channel stitching about 4 in. (10 cm) apart on front of top fabric. Pin layers together along marked lines. Sew along lines, extending stitching under border strips.

6 Pin pressed inner edges of border strips in place. Use medium straight stitches to edgestitch inner edges of border in place, sewing together top, batting, and lining.

Appliqués on Bedspreads

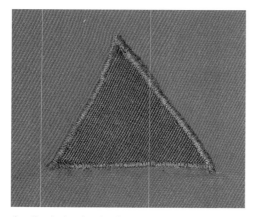

Appliqués in simple shapes add interest to a plain bedspread. Cut the appliqués from contrasting fabric and stitch around them with a close zigzag stitch.

Purchase an extra yard (90 cm) each of the top, lining, and border fabrics of your bedspread, or pick up the colors from elsewhere in the room, and make three coordinating accent pillows in simple geometric shapes.

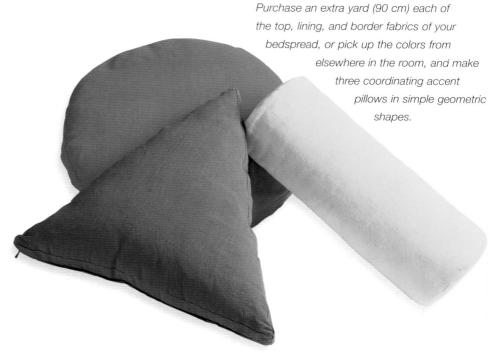

TRY THIS!

Beautifully crafted and decorated bed linens in crisp, fresh colors are a wonderful change from ordinary white sheeting. The reversible pillow and duvet covers shown were sewn from two linen fabrics in coordinating colors and stenciled with contrasting paint colors. You can create you own stencils and make them any shape that you like. Colorfast washable paints made especially for stenciling fabric are readily available in craft supply stores. Follow the manufacturer's instructions for applying and setting the paint and for laundering the painted fabric.

Quilting with Bows and Tassels

There are several ways to quilt a reversible bedspread that has batting placed between the top and lining. It can be stitched straight across the spread to create wide channels or stitched with many parallel lines for a striped effect. Sew across both horizontally and vertically to create a stitched plaid or checkerboard effect.

Because the bedspread is reversible, the stitches must look neat on both sides. Be sure the layers are pinned together at several places to prevent them from shifting as you are sewing.

An old-fashioned way of quilting is to stitch pieces of thin satin ribbons to one or both sides of the bedspread and tie them into small bows. You can also make small pom-pom tassels and stitch them onto the bedspread. Arrange and pin the bows or pom-poms over the whole spread before tacking them down.

Although it is traditional to use matching ribbons and yarn, contrasting colors can be used for a more contemporary look.

Create an heirloom-quality reversible bedspread by using fabrics of the same color but of different textures. For example, an off-white floral cotton damask can be backed with off-white satin for an elegant Victorian look.

Using Bows

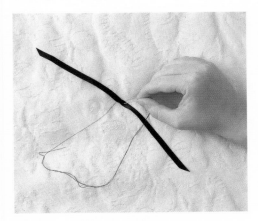

1 Cut an 8-in. (20-cm) length of narrow ribbon. Hand stitch center of ribbon in place, sewing through top, batting, and lining of bedspread.

2 Tie ends of ribbon into a small bow. Pull loops firmly when making bow to prevent it from coming undone. Baste bow in center for added security if desired. Trim ends even.

Using Pom-Pom Tassels

Wrap yarn many times around 1-in. (2.5-cm) cardboard square. Tie loops together at one end with piece of yarn; cut loops apart at other end. Draw one end of yarn tie through bedspread and back to top. Knot ends under pom-pom.

Colorful Bolster Pillows

A round bolster made with beautiful fabric and decorated with welting, a button, or a tassel is an attractive alternative to an ordinary throw pillow.

Bolsters are popular when a touch of elegance and comfort is called for. The foam form used is available wherever pillow forms are sold and is covered with polyester batting for softness.

Silk, velvet, and tapestry make rich coverings for bolsters used in the living room. Bedroom bolsters look luxurious in cotton fabric that matches the linens or in elegant satin that dresses up the bed beautifully.

Embellish the circular ends of the bolsters with matching or contrasting decorative trims.

Bolsters can be made from a single piece of fabric that wraps around the bolster form and is held at each end with a button. For additional accents of color, use separate pieces for the ends of the bolster and insert a contrasting welting within the seam.

A basic bolster cover is comprised of three elements: a rectangular piece of fabric for the body, which is sewn into a tube; two fabric sleeves for the ends; and a casing for the piping cord.

Measuring and Cutting

Be sure to measure the bolster form carefully, so the finished cover fits the form perfectly.

- Body = bolster's length + ½-in. (1-cm) seam allowance x circumference of bolster + 1¼ in. (3 cm) for zipper flap + ½-in. (1-cm) seam allowance. Cut one piece.
- Ends = half bolster's diameter + 1¼ in. (3 cm) for casing and seam allowance x bolster's circumference + ½-in. (1-cm) seam allowance. Cut two pieces.
- Welting = 1¼ in. (3 cm) x bolster's circumference + ½ in. (1 cm) seam allowance. Cut two pieces.

You'll Need:

- ✓ Foam bolster form
- ✓ Batting & gauze or cheesecloth to cover bolster form
- ✓ Coordinating fabrics for bolster-cover body, ends, & welting; matching threads
- ✓ 2 shank buttons or tassels
- ✓ Sewing machine with straight-stitch & zipper foot
- ✓ Zipper 1–2 in. (2.5–5 cm) shorter than bolster
- ✓ ½ in.-diameter cotton piping cord & #5 perle cotton thread
- ✓ Tape measure & scissors; safety & straight pins
- ✓ Iron & ironing board

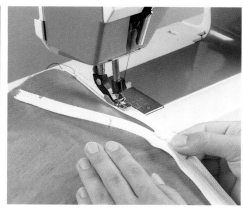

1 Open zipper. With right sides together, pin one zipper tape along one long edge of body piece. Using zipper foot, stitch along zipper guideline. Close zipper. Fold stitched edge of zipper to wrong side and press.

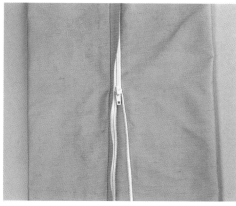

2 Fold opposite long edge 1¼ in. (3 cm) to wrong side; press. Place folded edge over closed zipper, aligning fold with stitched zipper line so zipper is hidden. Pin fabric to zipper; baste if desired. Sew on right side of fabric.

3 To make welting, fold welting strip in half, wrong sides facing. Insert cotton cording between layers next to fold. Using zipper foot, stitch as close to cord as possible for entire length of strip.

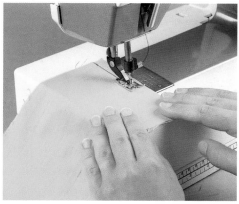

4 To make bolster ends, fold end piece in half crosswise with right sides facing. Sew short ends together to form a ring, leaving a ½-in. (1-cm) opening ½ in. (1 cm) from one end to insert gathering thread. Repeat for second bolster end.

5 To make casing for gathering bolster ends, press edge with opening ½ in. (1 cm) to wrong side twice. Edgestitch along inner edge of fold.

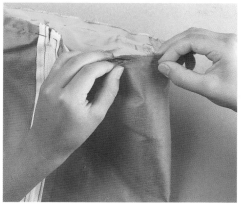

6 Pin welting to right side of body piece, raw edges even, and ends lapped across each other and in seam allowance. Pin right side of end piece to welting, matching all edges. Sew all layers together. Repeat for second end piece.

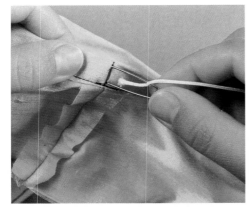

7 Pin perle cotton thread to safety pin. Close safety pin and insert into casing-seam opening; work pin and thread through entire casing and exit through same opening.

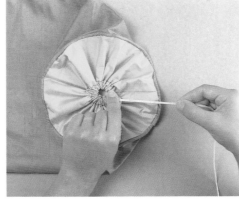

8 Pull ends of thread to gather hole closed. Tie ends securely; trim ends. Open zipper, then gather remaining end. Cut a length of perle cotton 6 in. (15 cm) longer than twice bolster length. Thread button onto perle cotton and fold in half.

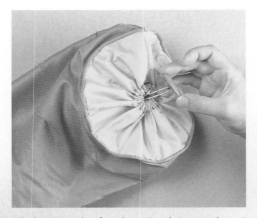

9 Insert ends of perle cotton into opening at bolster end; pull taut. Push one end of cotton thread through opposite opening; thread on second button; push end back into opening, pulling button tightly. Knot ends.

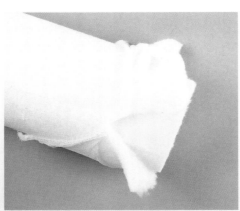

10 Cover full length of foam bolster with a layer of batting to soften shape. Wrap a piece of cotton gauze or cheesecloth over batting to hold; baste in place. Insert bolster into cover and close zipper.

Crafter's Corner

Instead of a firm foam bolster, make a soft headrest by tightly rolling up batting until the desired circumference is reached. Then wrap it tightly with cotton gauze or cheesecloth to hold its shape, baste, and insert into bolster cover.

TRY THIS!

Make a simple bolster cover from only one piece of fabric, then gather and tie the ends for a bolster that looks like a giant candy wrapper.

Cut the fabric to the length of the bolster plus 32 in. (80 cm). Sew the long ends together with a ¼-in. (5-mm) seam. Fold under ½ in. (1 cm) twice on each short end; press and hem. Center the bolster inside the cover, gather the ends, and tie with a ribbon or ties made from the same fabric.

Adding Lace Edgings to Bolster Ends

For a charming accessory to enhance your bedroom decor, make a bolster that is feminine yet unfussy by adding a ruffle of lace to flat, rather than gathered, end pieces.

Make a pattern for the flat end pieces by tracing around the bolster end or measuring the diameter of the bolster and drawing a circle with a compass. Then add a ¼-in. (5-mm) seam allowance all around.

You can also make a ruffled trim from the same fabric as the bolster cover. Cut a fabric strip slightly longer than twice the circumference of the bolster end and join ends to make a loop. Fold in half lengthwise, wrong sides together; gather to fit, then proceed with the basic directions for inserting a welting.

1 Cut and sew cover with a zipper following basic directions. Cut two end pieces, including seam allowance. With right sides together, pin and sew end pieces to cover.

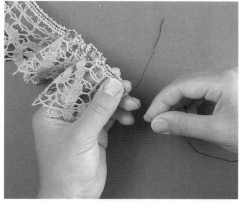

2 Cut a piece of lace edging slightly longer than twice the circumference of bolster. Sew a long running stitch along header edge of lace. Pull on thread to gather lace until it fits exactly around bolster's circumference.

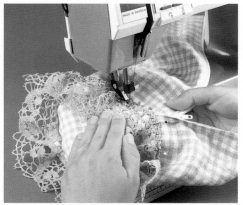

3 Pin gathered lace just above seam line of bolster's end, on right side of cover; edgestitch lace to cover. Baste lace ends together.

Lace edging to trim a bolster can be of any width, with edges that are finished straight, scalloped, or looped. Crocheted lace has a handmade look that fits a romantic country decor.

Cosmetic and Toiletry Bags

A cosmetic bag with an inner pocket and side handles makes a fabulous gift for that special traveler. Use it to hold personal items or as a storage container around the house.

Choose an attractive fabric for the outside in a pattern that suits the recipient. A handsome plaid, with its extension ends cut on the bias, is perfect for a business traveler, while a colorful, eye-popping design would suit a college-bound student. You can choose the perfect design for anyone.

Use a densely woven soil-and-stain-resistant fabric or a laminated (plastic-coated) fabric for the outside of the bag. For added strength, fuse a layer of fusible interfacing to the wrong side of the outer fabric.

The diamond-pattern cosmetics pouch was sewn from a moisture-resistant laminated fabric. To make the plush bag, cut out a semicircle with 7-in. (18-cm) diameter. Divide it into five wedges. Cut them from different-colored fabrics and join them to form two sides. Measure one curved edge to give the length of the 2-in. (5-cm) zipper gusset. Remember the seam allowances. Assemble, with piping, in a similar way to the other bags.

If liked, use moisture-resistant fabric (such as vinyl) or a tightly woven fabric (such as nylon flag fabric) for the lining and pocket.

Guidelines for Toiletry Bag

Cut following these directions, which include ½-in. (1-cm) seam allowances.

- From outer fabric and fusible interfacing, cut: a 11 x 17 in. (28 x 43 cm) piece for main body, two 3½ x 15¼ in. (9 x 38.7 cm) pieces for zipper gusset, and two 3½ x 6¼ in. (9 x 16 cm) pieces for gusset extensions.
- From outer fabric only, cut a 3½ x 12½ in. (9 x 31 cm) piece for handles.
- From lining fabric, cut: one 11 x 17 in. (28 x 43 cm) piece for main body; one 11 x 6 in. (28 x 15 cm) piece for pocket.
- To sew zipper gusset to main piece, mark center of each long edge of main body. Pin gusset and body together, right sides facing, so midpoints of gusset ends align with center markings of body. Stitch, clipping seam allowances as necessary around curves.

Cutting Guidelines for Pouch

The zipper on the cosmetics pouch is sewn directly to the top opening.

- From laminated fabric, cut one 14½ x 9½ in. (37 x 24 cm) piece, two 2½ x 5¼ in. (6 x 13 cm) gussets, and one 2¾ x 1¼ in. (7 x 3 cm) piece for zipper tab. Press under short edges of tab, then press in half.
- If desired, cut lining for main piece and gussets.

You'll Need:

✓ Fabrics: ½ yd. (45.7 cm) outer fabric & lining for bag; ⅜ yd. (34 cm) laminated fabric & lining (optional) for pouch

✓ Tape measure, scissors, & straight pins

✓ Sewing machine & matching thread; iron

✓ Zipper: 12 in. (30 cm) for bag; 9 in. (23 cm) for pouch

✓ 1¾ yds. (1.6 m) piping for bag; 2 yds. (1.8 m) double-fold tape for pouch

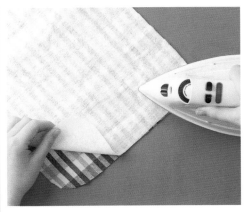

1 Cut out all fabric pieces. Cut and fuse lightweight interfacing to wrong side of main bag, zipper gussets, and gusset extension pieces. Fold main body piece in half and round corners.

3 If desired, pin tiny piece of fabric over ends of zipper tape to hold gusset edge at proper width. Pin one extension to one short edge of gusset, right sides facing; stitch. Sew remaining extension to opposite edge; press extensions out.

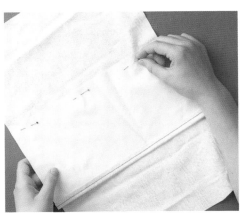

5 Stitch ¼ in. (5 mm) double hem along one long edge of lining pocket. Right sides facing, pin pocket to lining 6 in. (15 cm) down from one short edge with hemmed edge pointing down; stitch long raw edge. Bring hemmed edge of pocket up and press.

2 On one gusset piece, center one side of zipper, facedown, on right side of one long edge; stitch close to zipper teeth. Press zipper faceup. Stitch remaining gusset to opposite zipper edge in same way.

4 To make handles, fold long edges of strip to center, then fold in half lengthwise. Pin and stitch folded edges together; cut in half to make two handles. Lay handles across extension seams on gusset; stitch handle ends in place.

6 With wrong sides facing, pin lining to outer piece. Pin piping around edges on right side of bag, overlapping folded ends. Sew close to piping edge. Open zipper; pin and stitch gusset to body following guidelines; turn right side out.

Sewing a Cosmetic Pouch

1 If lining is being used, pin corresponding lining and laminated fabric pieces together, wrong sides facing. Encase one short edge of each gusset with double-fold binding tape.

2 Wrong sides facing, pin one long edge of main piece around one gusset piece; ends of main piece should extend higher than gusset pieces. Stitch together near raw edges. Encase raw edges in binding.

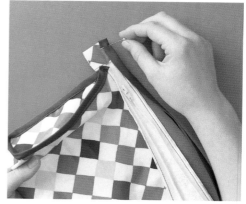

3 Wrong sides together, insert zipper at bag opening. Place zipper extension over top of zipper tape; stitch along its folded edges. Trim extension sides to match zipper width. Encase zipper edges with one continuous length of binding.

Crafter's Corner

Zippers come in a variety of lengths and are made with metal or plastic teeth or with nylon coils. Plastic or nylon is preferable if the zipper might get wet repeatedly.

If you need to shorten a zipper, determine the length you need and mark it on the closed zipper, measuring from the top stop down. At marking, whip-stitch repeatedly over the teeth, creating a new bar at the bottom to keep the zipper pull from coming off its track. Cut the zipper 1 in. (2.5 cm) below the whipstitching, insert the zipper as usual.

TRY THIS!

Nail clippers, nail files, and tweezers are best stored separately as they are sharp and pointed. Sew a special case for them with little pockets and straps. To prevent the points from going through the fabric, cut out some self-adhesive parchment and place it between the fabric layers.

Sew pockets and straps onto the inner fabric layer and then assemble bag and sew a zipper directly to entire edge. No gussets are needed because the case folds flat for storage.

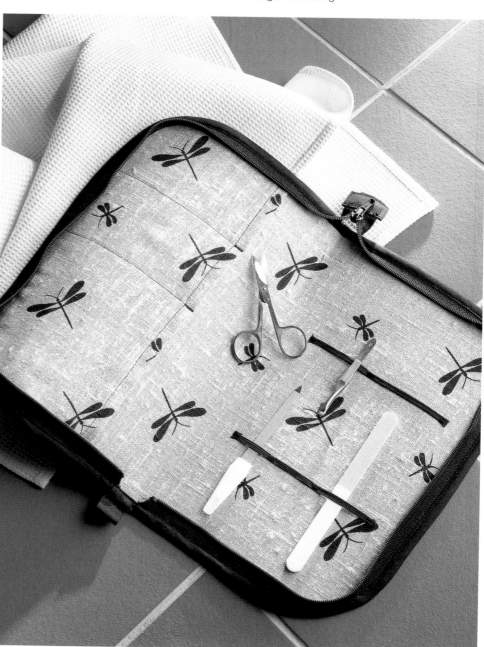

Sewing Fruit-shaped Cosmetic Bags

Sturdy fabrics with large, repeating motifs are ideal for making fun-shaped cosmetic bags and toiletry bags. Look for appropriate colorful patterns in fabric and home-decorating departments, such as this one with bold fruit motifs.

Begin by cutting out two identical fruit motifs for the sides. Add ½-in. (1-cm) seam allowance to all edges so the full outline of your motif will be visible after sewing. Based on the shape, figure out the length of the base, which should be at least 3 in. (7.5 cm) wide. Determine length of zipper you will need, then cut a base and two zipper gussets, adding ½-in. (1-cm) seam allowance all around pieces. Insert the zipper between the zipper gussets, then pin the zipper section to the side and base pieces.

The design of these delightful cosmetic pouches is determined by the motifs chosen from the printed fabric. Look for a similar type of print, so you can make a unique assortment of coordinating pouches. The laminated fabric makes them sturdy and waterproof, and allows for easy cleanup.

1 Follow outline of motifs to cut out two pieces for bag sides; add ½ in. (1 cm) for seam allowances. Cut out one base and two zipper gusset pieces, adding ½-in. (1-cm) seam allowance all around. Insert zipper between gusset pieces.

2 Pin short side of base piece to short end of zipper section, with right sides facing and edges aligned. Stitch, starting and stopping at seam line, not raw edges.

3 Pin bottom edge of motif to long side of base and sew in place. Repeat to attach second motif to other side of base. Pin and sew zipper section along top edge of each side motif; then join ends of zipper and base.

Embellished Pillow Covers

Button-front pillow covers offer stylish decorating options and, best of all, are easy to make. Vary the type of buttons and position of the closure to sew a set of covers for your pillows.

Pillow covers accented with functional and decorative button closures have a fresh, tailored look that blends with any decorating style. Suitable for all straight-sided pillows, the three-piece covers can be sewn with the buttons set straight or on a diagonal, as above.

The buttons should be chosen to complement the pillow fabric. Also shown above, novelty buttons lend an imaginative touch to a solid-colored cover, whereas simple buttons offset one made from a striped or print fabric.

A solid-colored button-tab closure adds detail to a tone-on-tone print pillow cover. A rectangular buttoned cover in the form of an envelope has a long back piece that folds over a shorter front piece and fastens with a horizontal row of buttons.

When selecting fabric for pillow covers, consider the wear the pillows will receive. If they are for a family room, select firmly woven, washable fabrics, preferably with a stain-resistant finish.

Choose any style button you desire, including two- or four-hole buttons, novelty-shaped and fabric-covered buttons. You can even combine buttons of different colors and shapes for a touch of whimsy.

Sewing Guidelines

The button-front of the pillow cover is made simply by overlapping two hemmed front pieces—one with buttonholes sewn along the overlap and the other with buttons sewn along the underlap.

- Cover can be adjusted to fit any size pillow: Cut back piece to dimensions of pillow plus 1 in. (2.5 cm). Cut two front pieces to pillow length plus 1 in. (2.5 cm) and half pillow width plus 4½–5 in. (11–13 cm).
- On one long side of each front piece, fold and stitch 1½-in. (4-cm) double hem to wrong side of fabric to create firm edge for button closure. If fabric is reversible, you can turn hems to right side of fabric (as shown at right) to create banded edge.
- Alternatively, closures can be fastened with ribbon or fabric ties, decorative studs, hidden snaps, and hooks and eyes.
- For envelope pillow, finish raw edges with zigzag stitch.

You'll Need:

- ✓ Decorator fabric
- ✓ Pillow form
- ✓ Buttons
- ✓ Tape measure, straight pins, & scissors
- ✓ Sewing machine with buttonhole attachment
- ✓ Hand-sewing needle & thread

Making a Center-Front Button Closure

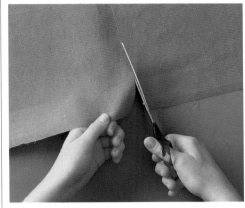

1 For 20-in. (50-cm) square finished pillow cover, cut one 21-in. 53-cm) square back piece and two front pieces measuring 14½ x 21 in. (37 x 53 cm), ½-in. (1-cm) seam allowances included.

2 Pin and press 1½-in. (4-cm) double hem to right side of fabric on inner long edge of both front pieces. Edgestitch along inner and outer folded edges. If desired, use contrasting-colored thread to show stitch details.

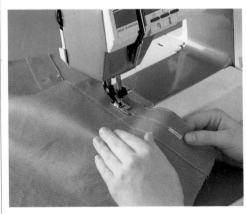

3 Stitch five evenly spaced buttonholes along center of one hemmed edge. Adjust size of buttonholes to buttons chosen. If using round buttons, make buttonholes ⅛ in. (3 mm) larger than diameter of buttons.

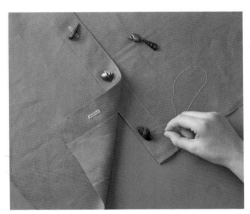

4 Overlap front pieces and mark position of buttons in corresponding positions along hemmed edge. Hand sew five buttons in marked positions. Button front pieces together.

5 Place buttoned front pieces and back piece together, right sides facing and edges aligned; pin. Stitch along edges with ½-in. (1-cm) seam.

6 Unbutton front piece and turn cover right side out. Push corners out. Insert pillow form in cover, then button front of cover closed.

Making an Envelope-Style Pillow Cover

1 To make 20-in. (50-cm) square finished cover, cut one 21 x 38 in. (53 x 96 cm) fabric piece for back of cover and foldover front extension. Cut one 21 x 24 in. (53 x 61 cm) piece for front of pillow cover, ½ in.-(1-cm) seam allowances included.

2 Fold one short side of back piece 12 in. (30 cm) to right side and pin; clip into side edges 6 in. (15 cm) from folded edge. Using ½-in. (1-cm) seams, stitch side edges from folded edge to clips. Fold one short edge of front piece 4 in. (10 cm) to wrong side; stitch fold.

3 Right sides together, pin front to back with fold of front edge at clip marks and under back flap. Sew three sides from one clip to other; turn right side out. Sew five buttonholes along top of flap; fold flap down. Sew buttons along front edge.

Crafter's Corner

Four-hole buttons can be machine stitched in place. Program your sewing machine to a zigzag stitch with the same width as the measurement between the holes in the button. Lower the feeder so the fabric remains stationary and does not move through the machine as the buttons are being sewn.

TRY THIS!

Make a pillow cover that buttons around all four sides. Simply cut two same-sized squares of fabric for the front and back and sew 1½-in. (4-cm) double hem along all four sides of each piece. Make buttonholes 1½ in. (4 cm) apart and 1 in. (2.5 cm) in from the edges of the top piece; sew the same number of buttons in corresponding positions along the edges of the bottom piece. If desired, stitch a smaller square of a complementary fabric to the front. Button the two squares together with a pillow form between them.

Sewing a Two-Cover Pillow

The center-buttoned pillow cover actually consists of two covers: a smaller inside cover that houses the pillow form and has a button sewn to its center; the larger outside cover that folds over the smaller one and fastens to the button with loops sewn into the corners. Both covers are made from two squares of fabric.

To determine the placement of the button, fold the cover piece into quarters, then mark the center point at the corner folds. Sew the button in place and then sew the cover pieces together. Before turning, trim the corner seam allowances to reduce bulk.

To assemble, insert the pillow into the smaller cover and slipstitch the opening closed. Slipstitch the opening of the larger outside cover. Place the covered pillow, button side up, centered diagonally on the outer cover. Fold the corners of the outer cover over the pillow and button.

The center-buttoned pillow cover looks very decorative with its crisscross layering and lively pattern play when made with two coordinating fabrics. Alternate the fabrics on the inner and outer covers for a stunning pillow pair.

1 Cut two 26½-in. (67-cm) squares and four 4-in.(10-cm) cords for outer cover. Loop cord; pin one to each corner on right side of one square. Sew squares, right sides facing, with ½-in. (1-cm) seam; leave opening. Turn right side out; slipstitch opening; press.

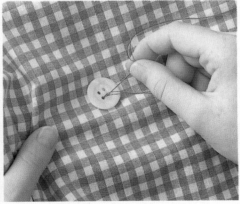

2 Cut two 20½-in. (52-cm) squares of fabric for inner cover. Fold one to mark center. Sew button to center. Pin pieces with right sides facing, edges aligned; stitch with ½-in. (1-cm) seam, leaving opening for turning. Turn right side out.

3 Insert pillow form into smaller cover. Slipstitch opening closed. With button face up, place pillow centered diagonally on larger, outside cover. Fold corners of outer cover over pillow and button loops at center.

Eye-catching Patchwork Quilts

Strips of scrap fabric joined to make these simple yet striking blocks create a clever and colorful patchwork quilt for your home.

Quilting has long been an American tradition. Warm blankets made up of fabric scraps offer both a economic and creative solution to one of life's absolute necessities.

Make your own quilt from either new fabrics or from pieces drawn from the scrap basket. Blend or contrast fabrics of various patterns and colors to create interesting variations for your quilt.

Consider coordinating a quilt with your interior by using fabric scraps left over from curtains and other projects. Be creative in composing your own designs.

Keep in mind the different effects of combining various color tones and fabric prints. Mix and match fabrics to create a sense of movement and texture across the surface of your quilt. Each block consists of a simple triangle, with the opposite side made up of strips of fabric sewn together.

It is best to use fabrics of a similar fiber content, such as 100% cotton fabrics that are easy to sew and can stand up to repeated washings. Prewash all fabrics before cutting out to avoid shrinkage and seam puckering. Sew with standard 100% cotton thread to match dominant color. Use ¼-in. (5-mm) seam allowances.

Finishing the Quilt

Each block is constructed separately with batting (polyester padding) and lining, then the blocks are joined. Adding wide border strips balances the quilt design. Borders 4–5 in. (10–13 cm) wide are effective frames.

- Cut batting and lining same size as borders. Baste batting to wrong side of borders, then baste lining to batting. Stitch borders to sides, then to top and bottom edges of quilt top.
- Measure finished quilt. Use as guide to cut backing (for underside of quilt) from coordinating fabric. If quilt top is wider than fabric width, piece fabric to obtain enough width for backing.
- Place backing right side up on flat surface. Lay quilt top, wrong side up, on backing. Pin layers together at edges, leaving opening for turning: (24 in. (60 cm) for larger quilts; 18 in. (45 cm) for smaller. Sew quilt top and backing together. Turn to right side; stitch opening closed. Stitch around blocks and borders.

1 To make block template, draw 12-in. (30- cm) square or desired block size on cardboard; add ½-in. (1-cm) seam allowance and cut out. Using template, cut batting and lining. Baste batting to lining 1 in. (2.5 cm) in from edges and across each diagonal.

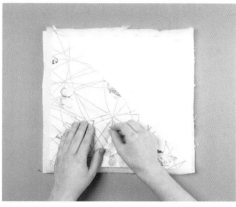

2 With pencil and ruler, connect two diagonal corners on batting. Cut 14 in. (35 cm) square from fabric. With pencil and ruler, connect two diagonal corners to make two triangles; cut out. Pin one triangle to batting square with edge ¼ in. (5 mm) across line.

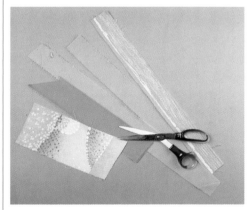

3 Cut five or six extra strips of varying widths and lengths along straight grain of fabric. Vary widths to between 1–2½ in. (2.5–6 cm); cut strips longer than needed to fit diagonally across square.

4 With right sides together, place first strip along long side of triangle, aligning raw edges. Pin in place. Stitch along diagonal with ¼-in. (5-mm) seam, sewing strip, triangle, batting, and lining together.

5 Unfold first strip so it lies flat against batting. Press flat. Place second strip along first strip, raw edges even and right sides facing. Pin and stitch.

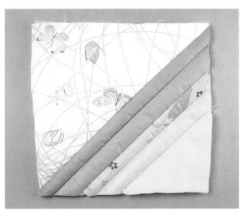

6 Continue adding strips until block is covered. Make 41 more blocks in same manner, using selected fabric colors and patterns and varying strip widths.

7 Trim ½ in. (1 cm) from cardboard template. Place template over each block. Align cardboard corners with triangle corners. Trace around template with pencil to even out block outline.

8 Carefully cut along pencil marks to make edges even. As alternative, use rotary cutter instead of scissors: Place block on self-healing cutting mat. Holding cutter upright and against cardboard template, cut out block.

9 Stitch through all layers by hand or machine along all edges to hold block pieces together for joining. Arrange blocks into six rows of seven blocks each, strips and diagonals all in same direction.

10 Right sides facing, join blocks togther with ¼-in. (5-mm) seams. Carefully trim seams at intersecting corners to reduce bulk. Add the borders and complete the quilt as instructed on page 181.

TRY THIS!

This quilt-making technique is attractive both in smaller and larger formats, so don't limit your creativity to large quilts. For a quick project, try making a pillow. You need only the tiniest scraps of fabric to make a pillow with small 2-in. (5-cm) blocks, or any small size you wish. Complement the dominant color scheme of your room by blending fabrics of the same color intensity but of different hues. For a striking pillow, select a strong solid contrast color for the triangles, and brights for the strips. Choose a background fabric in a solid color or a small print, letting the fabric strips define the design. Arrange blocks in alternate directions to form a pinwheel effect.

Crafter's Corner

When collecting fabrics for quilting, check your local fabric store for remnants, or try recycling old clothing or other items made from interesting materials. Gather fabrics of the same weight and with the same laundering and ironing requirements. Wash all fabrics before to preshrink and remove sizing. Test colorfastness by wiping a corner of the wet fabric across a white strip. If colors bleed, set them in a mixture of one part white vinegar and three parts cold water. Rinse until water runs clear. Press before cutting out.

Creating Patchwork Quilt Designs

One simple patchwork block can be the basis for a surprising number of different quilts. Changing the arrangement of the blocks leads to an exciting number of possibilites.

It is always best to plan a patchwork design ahead of time. The end results are well worth the extra effort. First, experiment with different color compositions for each block. Begin by drawing several outlines of the block onto graph paper, and use colored pencils to fill in the designs, trying several different color combinations. Use the drawings as a reference for sewing the blocks together.

Once you plan the arrangement of the individual blocks, design the quilt top. Cut out the blocks and join them in various positions in order to visualize what the completed quilt will look like. Be creative and try as many different options as possible before settling on an arrangement. Sew the blocks together only when you are completely satisfied with the design.

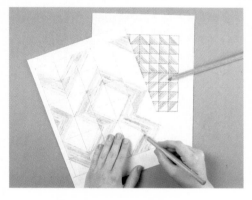

The most exciting part of quilt making is choosing the color scheme and arrangement of the blocks, and watching the final results as each block comes together. The arrangement above results in a large zigzag motif. For a more traditional look, blocks can be arranged into a repeating pattern where all the striped triangles face the same direction. Or the striped triangles can be turned toward each other to form a pattern of diamonds.

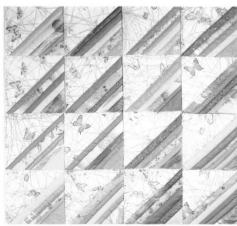

Loose Slipcovers

Reupholstering a sofa can be difficult and time-consuming. But with these loose slipcovers, refreshing a tired, old sofa has never been easier.

A sofa that is still comfortable to sit in but has a tattered or outdated covering is well worth renewing. However, the task of sewing form-fitting upholstery can be a daunting one. This loose-fitting slipcover is an easy and inexpensive solution.

Made from straight pieces of cut fabric, the cover requires a minimal amount of sewing and is shaped and held in place with attached fabric strips tied into pretty bows at strategic points on the sofa. Untie the bows to remove the cover for laundering or a change in decor. This way you can change the look of your room in an instant.

Cinch in the excess fabric on the front of the armrest by lacing cord through grommets or by tying a large fabric bow. Lend a lively informality to the overall look of the sofa by combining complementary fabrics, such as the check bows and colorful plaid armrest on this plain pink slipcover.

Even if you are a novice sewer, you can make this custom-tailored slipcover, which consists of a large main piece of fabric sewn to two rectangular pieces that cover the armrests and sides. The fabric is held fast between the seat and back pillows by an encased dowel. Fabric ties at the front of the armrests and at the top and back of the sofa help shape the loosely fitted cover. When the slipcover needs laundering, it can be easily removed.

General Guidelines

For best results, use a densely woven, sturdy cotton or linen fabric that is less likely to shift after the cover is assembled.

- If fabric has been treated with soil-resistant finish, do not prewash. Otherwise, wash fabric before cutting.
- If you purchase fabric from standard 45 in. (1.15m) - or 54 in. (1.37m)-wide bolts, you may need to piece panels to achieve required width.
- Alternatively, use densely woven cotton or cotton-blend sheets. Two king-size sheets are sufficient to cover average-size sofa.
- To make ties, cut twelve 9 x 49 in. (23 x 124.5 cm) fabric strips. Fold each in half lengthwise, right sides facing; sew long edges and one short edge. Turn right side out and press flat.

You'll Need:

✓ Sofa

✓ Fabric cut to sofa measurements plus extra 3½ yd. (3.2 m) for ties

✓ ¾ in. (2 cm) dowel, cut to fit across seat cushions

✓ Tape measure, fabric marker, scissors & pins

✓ Sewing machine & thread

✓ Grommets & decorative cord for laced sofa

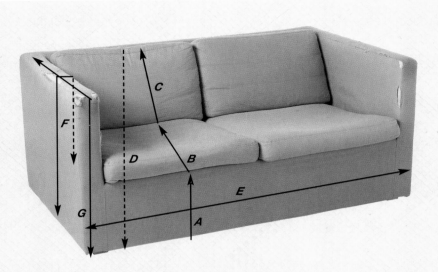

Measuring and cutting

Length of main cover piece = A + B + C + D; width of main cover piece = E
Length of armrest piece = F; width of armrest piece = G

Measuring sofa for main cover piece: To determine length of main cover piece, measure sofa from bottom of sofa front (A), back across seat (B), up backrest (C), then down back to bottom of floor (D). To determine width, measure sofa from outermost edge to outermost edge (E).

Measuring sofa for armrest piece: To determine length of armrest piece, measure up side of armrest, over the top, and down inner side to seat (F). To determine width, measure from bottom of armrest, up and along armrest top (G).

After taking sofa measurements, add 8 in. (20 cm) all around for seam allowances, hems, and tuck in allowances. Cut the fabric so the lengthwise grain runs from front to back on the main piece and from the bottom of the armrest side to the seat for the armrest piece. Seam panels together, if necessary, to obtain proper dimensions for each piece.

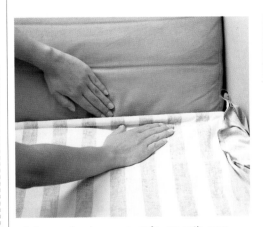

1 Lay main piece over sofa; smooth over seat and back so there is same amount of excess at bottom of front and back. Mark where seat meets backrest. Remove piece and sew 1 in. (2.5 cm) casing at mark. Insert dowel. Replace fabric to check fit.

2 With right sides facing, sew armrest piece to side of main piece from bottom edge up to casing. Place covering on sofa, pushing dowel between seat and backrest and tucking fabric snugly between armrest and seat and armrest and backrest.